D0041812

J. D. Salinger:

The Catcher in the Rye and Other Works

ished on July 16, 1951. It is the story of an upper-mid

1951. It is the story of an upper-middle-class, urban, sixt

J. D. Salinger:

The Catcher in the Rye and Other

Raychel Haugrud Reiff

Marshall Cavendish Benchmark
New York

Marshall Cavendish Benchmark
99 White Plains Road
Tarrytown, NY 10591
www.marshallcavendish.us

Library of Congress Cataloging-in-Publication Data
Reiff, Raychel Haugrud.
J.D. Salinger : the Catcher in the Rye and other works / by Raychel Haugrud Reiff.
p. cm. — (Writers and their works)
Summary: "A biography of writer J. D. Salinger that describes his era, his major works--especially The Catcher in the Rye, his life,
and the legacy of his writing"—Provided by publisher.
Includes bibliographical references and index.
ISBN-13: 978-0-7614-2594-6
1. Salinger, J. D. (Jerome David), 1919- 2. Authors, American—20th century—Biography. I. Title. II. Series.
PS3537.A426Z845 2007
813'.54—dc22
[B] 2006019236

All quotations are cited in the text. Notes containing additional information and sources are included at the back of this book.

Photo research by Linda Sykes Picture Research, Inc., Hilton Head, SC

The Lotte Jacobi Collection, University of New Hampshire: Cover, 2, 6;
Private Collection: 10; Courtesy YMCA: 12; The Granger Collection: 18, 45, 47, 54; Bettmann/Corbis: 28, 60, 107; Everett Collection: 34; Rick Maiman/Corbis Sygma: 37 top; ©The New York Times: 37 bottom; The Advertising Archive: 56; Paul Colangelo/Corbis: 65; Rare Books and Special Collections, Princeton University Library: 82; Getty Images: 100; AP/Wide World Photos: 108.

Publisher: Michelle Bisson
Art Director: Anahid Hamparian
Designer: Sonia Chaghatzbanian

Printed in China
1 3 5 6 4 2

Contents

ished on July 16, 1951. It is the story of an upper-mid
s, urban, sixteen-year-old male who in 1949 or 1950 jour
ew York after being expelled from school, and particip
chaotic, bleak adult world. Holden Caulfield relates fo

-old male who in 1949 or 1950 journeys to New York after be
lled from school, and participates in a chaotic, bleak ad
d. Holden Caulfield relates forty-eight hours in his l
ribing his pessimistic attitudes about society and the wo
e thinks about sex, adults, and American values. *The Cat*
he *Rye*, Salinger's only published novel, WAS published on
951. It is the story of an upper-middle-class, urban, sixt
-old male who in 1949 or 1950 journeys to New York after be
lled from school, and participates in a chaotic, bleak ad
d. Holden Caulfield relates forty-eight hours in his l
ribing his pessimistic attitudes about society and the wo
e thinks about sex, adults, and American values. *The Cat*
he *Rye*, Salinger's only published novel, WAS published on
951. It is the story of an upper-middle-class, urban, sixt

Introduction

JEROME DAVID (J. D.) SALINGER has created two myths that have fascinated readers and critics for over half a century: Holden Caulfield and J. D. Salinger. Born in New York City on New Year's Day in 1919, Salinger grew up between the two world wars, fought in major battles in World War II, and became a serious short-story writer in the late 1940s. His chief claim to fame is his one novel, *The Catcher in the Rye,* published in 1951. Two years later, he collected some of his earlier stories into one volume called *Nine Stories.* Later, he combined four of his five stories written after *Catcher* into two books: *Franny and Zooey* (1961) and *Raise High the Roof Beam, Carpenters and Seymour: An Introduction* (1963). Although somewhat popular with the same readers who admire Salinger's novel, these last stories are not seen as equal to *The Catcher in the Rye.* The creation of Holden Caulfield is Salinger's crowning achievement. Although reviews were mixed when the book appeared, the obscene language was criticized from the beginning. As the novel increased in popularity and was placed on high school reading lists, many adults called for it to be banned. Nevertheless, the novel continued to sell well and to touch the lives of a wide variety of readers. Salinger's second myth, the legend of his own life, has enthralled people for decades, even though he has not published any work since 1965. He is one of the most famous literary recluses, withdrawing from the public eye to live in the hills of Cornish, New Hampshire, in 1953. Since then he has rarely granted interviews or made public appearances, finding fame, publicity, and literary criticism abhorrent. Although the myth of J. D. Salinger has been partially eroded by recent biographies and memoirs, the myth of Holden Caulfield remains. He will always be the sixteen-year-old whose sense of alienation in a phony, corrupt world speaks to readers worldwide. *The Catcher in the Rye* remains one of the most popular and widely read works of modern literature.

Chapter 1

The Life of J. D. Salinger

AS A YOUNG MAN, J. D. Salinger led an exciting life, filled with successes and adventures most people only dream of, and perils most people only encounter in their worst nightmares. By his mid-thirties, Salinger was personally acquainted with some of the greatest American writers of twentieth-century literature, including Ernest Hemingway and Eugene O'Neill. He had achieved national fame with his short stories and international celebrity with his novel. Further renown came to him when one of his short stories was adapted into a major Hollywood movie, *My Foolish Heart*. The sales of his work led to financial independence. He traveled internationally, and lived in Austria and Poland in the late 1930s, leaving Austria just before Hitler and the Nazi forces took over the country in March 1938. He toured Canada in 1940, visited the British Isles in 1951, and traveled in Mexico in 1952. He took part in some of the major historical events of the twentieth century: he stormed the beaches of Normandy on D-day in World War II, fought in the Battle of the Bulge, and interrogated Nazi war criminals. Salinger was definitely an important man-of-the-world, who seemed to be living the American dream. But on his thirty-fourth birthday, January 1, 1953, Salinger gave up a life of excitement, privilege, fame, and glamour in New York City, retired to a cottage in the hills of New Hampshire, and began living a life of quiet seclusion.

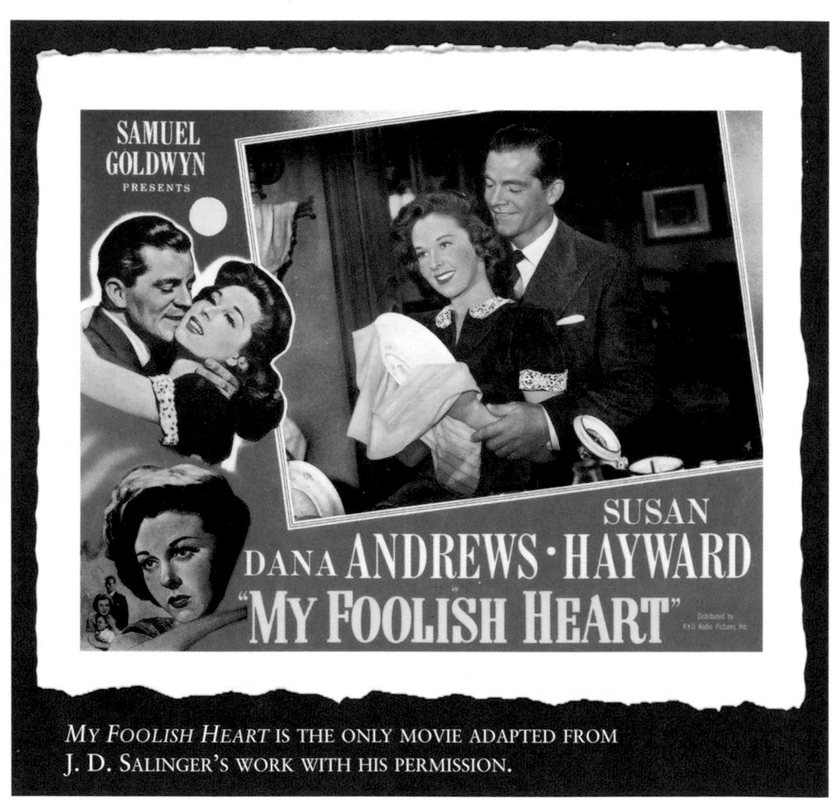

My Foolish Heart is the only movie adapted from J. D. Salinger's work with his permission.

Growing Up

Born on January 1, 1919, in New York City, Jerome David Salinger was welcomed as the only son of Solomon (called Sol) and Miriam Salinger. His sister, Doris, six years his elder, remembers how the entire family fawned over the little boy, whom they nicknamed "Salinger": "Mother doted on him, he could do no wrong. I thought he was perfect, too." (Margaret Salinger, 17)

Not much is known about the backgrounds of Sol and Miriam Salinger. Even their children, although acquainted with their Salinger relatives, did not know their maternal relations. Doris thinks their mother, born in Iowa or Ohio, met twenty-two-year-old Solomon Salinger at a county fair in Ohio when she was seventeen, fell in love at first sight, and later eloped. But since Sol was Jewish and Miriam, whose birth name was Marie Jillich, was Irish Catholic, it appears that Marie's family disowned her, for she never spoke of them. Once Marie married, she changed her name to the more Jewish sounding "Miriam," an Old Testament name, and passed as a Jew.

The young couple lived in poverty in Chicago, where Sol managed a movie theater and Miriam sold tickets and concessions. When Sol got a job in the meat and cheese import business with J. S. Hoffman and Company in Chicago, their financial situation improved. Soon, Sol was promoted to manager of the New York office. When Salinger was born, the family lived in northern Harlem, but within the year, they moved to a more fashionable neighborhood on the Upper West Side near Columbia University. In the next few years, as Sol made more money, the family continued moving south into more affluent neighborhoods. By the time Salinger was nine, they lived near Central Park.

Sol and Miriam were generous parents, giving their children privileged lives of leisure and culture. At a young age, Salinger was introduced to the literary and artistic

J. D. Salinger's parents sent him to the prestigious McBurney School in Manhattan as soon as they had the money to do so.

world. He was a regular visitor to the Metropolitan Museum of Art and the American Museum of Natural History and a frequent attendee of Broadway plays and movies. During summer vacations, the Salingers sent their son to summer camps. With his interest in films and plays, he loved to act, and when he was eleven, he was voted "most popular actor" at Camp Wigwam in Harrison, Maine. (Skow, 11) The family also took summer vacations at the beach, where Sol played in the waves with his young children.

Salinger attended public schools for eight years on Manhattan's Upper West Side. There, he was a reporter for the school paper, the manager of the fencing team, and an actor in two plays, where he was recognized as "good in public speaking." (Lutz, 9–10) With an IQ of 104 and grades of mostly Bs, Salinger was average in ability but "poor" in deportment. (Alexander, 33)

Sol kept making money as an importer of luxury foods, even when the rest of the country was struggling through the Great Depression of the 1930s. In 1932, the family moved to a spacious apartment on Park Avenue in the Upper East Side, an affluent, non-Jewish neighborhood near the Metropolitan Museum of Art. Now well-off, Sol and Miriam enrolled their thirteen-year-old son in the famous McBurney School, a private Young Men's Christian Association School in Manhattan. This was not a movement away from the Jewish religion, since the Salingers, like many nonreligious or secular Jews, did not attend Jewish religious services and even celebrated Christmas.

Even though he attended a Christian school, Salinger still followed the Jewish custom of having a bar mitzvah, a coming-of-age ceremony, in 1933, when he was fourteen—one year later than traditional. Shortly after, Sol and Miriam told Salinger and Doris that their mother was not Jewish, a devastating blow to both children. Doris explained to her niece, "It wasn't nice to be part Jewish in those days. It was no asset to be Jewish either, but at least you belonged somewhere." (Margaret Salinger, 24) Growing up as a Jewish American in the 1920s and 1930s was hard due to widespread discrimination against Jews. In fact, many buildings and areas in New York were restricted, with signs that read: "No Catholics, Jews, or dogs allowed." (Margaret Salinger, 28) Even major magazines like the *Saturday Evening Post* contributed to the prejudice, calling Polish Jews (such as Sol Salinger) "human parasites . . . mongoloids not fit to govern themselves." (quoted in Lutz, 8) For the rest of his life, Salinger was bothered by the fact that he was only half-Jewish, and many of his conflicted fictional characters are children of Jewish/Gentile parents.

Shortly after this revelation, Salinger started having academic trouble at McBurney, which his daughter, Margaret Ann (called Peggy) thinks was a direct result of this discovery, although the school records state that he was "hard hit by adolescence" (Ian Hamilton, 22; Margaret Salinger, 30) and that "he did not know the meaning of the word 'industry.'" (Lutz, 10) Salinger's academic performance was so poor that at the end of his sophomore year in 1934, he flunked out of McBurney. Although he took summer classes at the Manhassat School in an effort to make up his poor grades, he performed poorly and had to find a new school.

That fall he enrolled as a junior at Valley Forge Military Academy in Wayne, Pennsylvania, the model for Pencey Prep in *The Catcher in the Rye*. At this time the teenager decided to stop using the name "Jerome," informing his family and friends that he would now be called "Jerry." (Alexander, 39)

His time at military school, unlike Holden Caulfield's boarding school, was quite happy in spite of the school's location in central Pennsylvania, "which was rated by a U.S. Army war board survey as an epicenter of anti-Semitism in America." (Margaret Salinger, 30; Lutz, 10) The resulting anti-Jewish feelings were "hell on Salinger."

(Margaret Salinger, 30) Eagerly, Salinger participated in a number of activities. He acted in plays; worked for the fencing team, losing the team's equipment on the subway, just like Holden; (Margaret Salinger, 33) sang with the Glee Club; and belonged to the Aviation, French, and Noncommissioned Officers clubs. In his senior year, he was the literary editor of the yearbook, *Crossed Sabres,* and he wrote a poem that became the school's song. At Valley Forge, he began his writing career, composing stories at night, tenting a blanket over his head so no one would see his flashlight after the lights were supposed to be out.

Though not as rebellious as Holden Caulfield, Salinger did break school rules—getting drunk, sneaking into town to have an early breakfast and hot chocolate, and secretly swimming at an adjoining estate when the owners were gone.

Preparing for a Career

After graduating from Valley Forge in June 1936, Salinger spent the next five years rather aimlessly trying to decide what to do with his life. Financially supported by his parents, he drifted in and out of colleges, struggled to get a job as an actor, briefly attempted to learn his father's business, and tried to establish himself as a writer.

Attending College and Searching for Acting Jobs

After his high school graduation, Salinger knew he wanted to be a writer. Although Mrs. Salinger fully supported her son, Mr. Salinger, who was more practical, worried that writing would not provide an adequate income. He wanted his son either to go to college to learn a profession or to enter the family import business, which caused Salinger to feel that his father was a "dope." (Margaret Salinger, 34) Salinger enrolled at the expensive New York University in the fall of 1936. But, unwilling to apply himself at college, he dropped out of NYU sometime in the second semester of his freshman year to try to become an actor.

His Valley Forge classmate, Herbert Kauffman, relates that in 1937, he and Salinger "used to do the rounds of New York theaters, each hoping for a break." (Ian Hamilton, 38) But when they failed to land acting jobs, they worked for a few weeks as "entertainers" on a cruise ship, the Swedish liner *MS Kungsholm*, where they organized games and served as dancing partners to single women.

Learning the Family Business

By late 1937, Salinger, having quit his job on the ship, was ready to try to learn the family business. Thus, he and his father traveled to Europe. Beginning in Vienna, Salinger stayed with a Jewish family he grew to love; he left in early 1938, about a month before Austria fell to Hitler. (His ties to his Viennese family were completely severed several years later because the entire family was killed by the Nazis.) Next, he traveled to Poland to learn the meat industry but, repulsed by pig slaughtering, decided never to go into the family business. Almost immediately, in spring 1938, he returned to the United States and moved in with his parents. Nothing was ever said again about Salinger joining the family business.

Attempting College Again

That fall, he decided to go to college once again, this time enrolling as a freshman at Ursinus College in Collegeville, Pennsylvania. Although "most" of the girls were "mad about . . . this handsome, suave, and sophisticated New Yorker" and "enchanted by his biting and acerbic manner," most of his fellow students remember him as "bored and unhappy," a "loner" who "looked on the college and the students with disdain." "Nasty" and "caustic," he "never smiled, gave a friendly greeting or responded to overtures of acceptance." (quoted in Ian Hamilton, 44–45) Unlike most students at Ursinus College who felt privileged to receive a higher education during the Depression years of the 1930s, the wealthy New Yorker looked upon college as a way to pass time. After one semester, he quit school and returned to New York to live with his parents.

Becoming a Writer

Wanting to learn how to develop his literary skills, the twenty-year-old Salinger, in the spring of 1939, audited a Friday evening short-story writing class at Columbia University taught by Whit Burnett, the well-known editor of the magazine *Story*, an important publication for new writers. Burnett remembers Salinger as a dark-eyed young man who sat in class "without taking notes, seemingly not listening, looking out the window." (Alexander, 55) After doing nothing during the spring semester, Salinger audited the class for a second time in the fall, once again daydreaming throughout most of the course. Then, suddenly, he wrote a good story, "The Young Folks," which Burnett published in *Story* in the March/April issue of 1940. Salinger's first published story earned him twenty-five dollars.

After spending the summer traveling in Cape Cod and Canada, Salinger returned to his parents' home in New York in the fall and seriously began writing stories, intent on making a living as a writer. This was not an idle dream, for in the 1930s and 1940s, national magazines such as the *Saturday Evening Post* and *Collier's* paid $2,000 (about $27,000 in today's currency) for a story. (Margaret Salinger, 40) That September, he decided that he would no longer publish under his first name, "Jerome," a name he found ugly, or his middle name, "David," which he thought was a "terrible name" because it was too "Jewish-sounding." (Margaret Salinger, 27) At this point, he did not seem to want to be identified as Jewish, and started signing his stories "J. D. Salinger."

He kept trying to get his stories published and did not give up even though the rejection slips mounted. He succeeded in getting a second story printed in 1940; "Go See

SALINGER WAS PART OF THE AMERICAN INVASION OF NORMANDY ON D-DAY, JUNE 6, 1944. THAT DAY CHANGED THE COURSE OF WORLD WAR II AND OF SALINGER'S LIFE.

Eddie" appeared in the prestigious but nonpaying *University of Kansas City Review* in December. In 1941, Salinger achieved some financial success when he sold three stories to well-paying national magazines (*Collier's, Esquire,* the *New Yorker*). Romance was also part of his life in 1941. Salinger, at age twenty-two, was dating Oona O'Neill, the beautiful sixteen-year-old daughter of writer Eugene O'Neill.

Experiencing the Horrors of War

While Salinger was busy writing stories in New York in the late 1930s and early 1940s, war was raging in Europe. When the Japanese bombed Pearl Harbor on December 7, 1941, America entered World War II. The twenty-three-year-old Salinger was drafted into the U.S. Army; his first day was April 27, 1942.

Training

For the next two years he remained in America, training for war. In Maryland, he received special training as an agent of the Army Counterintelligence Corps. While Salinger was in Georgia in 1943, eighteen-year-old Oona broke his heart by ending their romance and marrying fifty-four-year-old Charlie Chaplin; Salinger found their union disgusting. During these years he continued writing and publishing stories. Although he was paid little money for the work published in *Story*, he received $2,000 for his story in *Collier's* and for each of his four stories in the *Saturday Evening Post*. Many of his early works were patriotic, glorifying the necessity of war to counteract evil. However, his attitude changed dramatically after he participated in combat.

Staff Sergeant Salinger's final training began in March 1944, when he was shipped to England to get ready for D-day, the date the Allied forces launched the largest military air and sea invasion in human history in an effort to stop Hitler's powerful Nazi forces.

Fighting

From D-day on June 6, 1944, to V-E (Victory in Europe) day on May 7, 1945, Staff Sergeant Jerome Salinger fought the Nazis on or near the front lines as one of two special counterintelligence agents with the Twelfth Infantry Regiment of the Fourth Division, never missing a day of service.

The action began for Sergeant Salinger on Utah Beach, Normandy, France, on D-day. After wading 200 feet to shore while being bombarded by German gunmen, Salinger's division faced a hellish open beach of burning equipment, dead and wounded soldiers, crashing mortars, and deadly fire from machine guns. The horrors of the day remained with Salinger forever. Although he never talked about specific details of the invasion, he often told his daughter Peggy, "I landed on D-day, you know." (Margaret Salinger, 53)

For the next year, Salinger fought the Nazis, a group of people he hated not only because he was a patriotic American whose country was at war with the Germans, but also because his personal life was constantly threatened by them. In June, he survived the Nazi ambushes in the Battle of the Hedgerows, but 76 percent of the officers in Salinger's infantry and 63 percent of its enlisted men had been killed or wounded. (Johnson, 119) Salinger wrote a letter to Whit Burnett on June 28, telling his mentor that he was unable to "describe the events of the past three or four weeks" because they were "too horrendous to put into words." (Alexander, 96).

During the next two months, Salinger and his unit fought their way to Paris, often gaining only a few hundred yards, the length of two or three football fields, in a day. When they entered Paris on August 25, they were warmly greeted as the liberators of Paris, one of the few joyous moments of the war for Salinger. During the couple of days he spent there, Salinger was able to meet Ernest Hemingway, who, at Salinger's request, read one of the stories Salinger had written and was favorably impressed. (Baker, 533)

Salinger's unit spent the fall driving the Germans back through France and Belgium. At Hürtgen Forest, Salinger and his unit fought in a savage battle that historian Stephen E. Ambrose calls "grossly, even criminally stupid . . . fought under conditions as bad as American soldiers ever had to face." (Victors, 266) The suffering endured by Salinger and the other men was immense. In subzero temperatures, the men sought shelter in ice-lined foxholes, rectangular holes 4 to 5 feet deep, 2 to 3 feet wide, and 6 feet long, dug in the ground. When the temperatures rose above freezing, the holes filled with 2 to 20 inches of water, and the men's leather boots soaked up the icy water, causing them to suffer from trench foot. Throughout his life, Salinger credited his mother with saving him because every week she sent him gifts of knitted socks; since he was able to keep his feet dry, he did not develop trench foot. (Margaret Salinger, 65) After a month of violent fighting, Salinger's Twelfth Infantry had possession of its portion of the Hürtgen Forest.

Salinger's regiment was next sent to Luxembourg to fight in the Battle of the Bulge. When the Nazis surrounded the town of Echternach on December 16, Salinger's friends and family feared he had died until Mrs. Salinger received a call on December 26 telling her that "Salinger is all right." (Margaret Salinger, 66)

In the early months of 1945, Salinger's division advanced deeper into Germany, capturing towns quickly. As part of the counterintelligence group, Salinger arrested Nazis, sealed up party buildings, and investigated suspicious Germans. By May 8, 1945, Germany had surrendered, and V-E day was celebrated. After eleven months of almost constant fighting, Salinger's regiment was through with battles. Salinger won five battle stars for his service.

During this year of battles, Salinger continued writing, carrying a portable typewriter in his Jeep. Instead of writing to his family, like most GIs, Salinger "spent much of his time sending letters, postcards, and manuscripts to magazine editors." (Lutz, 4) One of his army acquaintances "remembers him typing away, crouching under a table, while his area was under attack." (Skow, 13–14) In a communication to Whit Burnett, Salinger wrote: "Am still writing whenever I can find the time and an unoccupied foxhole." (quoted in Lutz, 4) The stories written during this year show an abrupt change in his feelings about war. For example, "A Boy in France," published in the *Saturday Evening Post* on March 31, 1945, is the story of a homesick, lonely GI in a foxhole in France. Salinger published more stories in 1945 than in any year except 1948. Although they were commercial successes, appearing in such popular magazines as *Cosmopolitan, Saturday Evening Post,* and *Esquire,* most critics find the stories largely forgettable. Salinger himself did not want these stories reprinted because he did not "think they're worthy of publishing." (quoted in Alexander, 250)

Breaking Down

With the fighting over, Salinger, as a counterintelligence officer, quickly learned the horrors of the Nazi regime as he entered the concentration camps and worked at the Nuremberg trials. His body finally caved in early summer 1945, and he was hospitalized outside Nuremberg for what was termed "battle fatigue," a euphemism for a nervous breakdown. After a few weeks of hospitalization, Salinger returned to active duty and continued bringing in suspected Nazis for interrogation.

Effects of the War

Salinger remained affected by the horrors of war throughout his life, but, strangely, the Holocaust did not seem to disturb this half-Jewish man. No references exist to show that Salinger had any response to the Holocaust. However, his years as a soldier profoundly influenced his creative life. Critics such as James E. Miller Jr. feel "that the war was responsible for, or at least brought to the surface, an alienation from modern existence so profound as to manifest itself at times in an overpowering spiritual nausea." (Miller, 6) Biographer James Lundquist agrees, writing that even though Salinger's stories are not truly war stories, nevertheless, the war created a mood in him "of loneliness, isolation, ineffectuality, and a sense of being a misfit in an unfit society." (Lundquist, 3)

The war also affected his personal life. His daughter relates that although she did not know her father was a writer when she was young, she always knew he was a soldier, for the war was "often in the foreground of our family life" and "always in the background. . . . It was the point of reference that defined everything else in relation to it." (Margaret Salinger, 44) His stories, his clothes, his regulation-style hair cut, his bent nose from diving out of a jeep while being shot at, his deaf ear from an explosion of a mortar shell, his Jeep that he drove as if he were dodging bullets, his guns, his GI watch, his cans of emergency supplies and army surplus water stored in the cellar, his medals, and his good friend, John Keenan, who was his Jeep partner during the war, were all reminders that her father was a soldier. (Margaret Salinger, 43)

Mentally, also, the war remained with Salinger. Peggy remembers standing next to him when she was about seven, watching him stare at the strong bodies of the young boys constructing the new addition to their house. After a long time, he said, "'All those big strong boys' . . . always on the front line, always the first to be killed, wave after wave of them' . . . his hand [was] flat, palm out, pushing arc-like waves away from him." (Margaret Salinger, 60)

At the close of the war, Salinger suffered "profound despair" because of his war experiences. (Maynard, 334) Afraid he would lose his mind, he thought he should get married "if only to steady his nerves." (Maynard, 334) And that is what he did.

Marrying Sylvia

Not much is known about his first wife, Sylvia, who was some sort of doctor. Although a number of critics have described her as French, (Hamilton, 97; Alexander, 109; French, *J. D. Salinger,* 25) Salinger's daughter says that she was German. According to Salinger's sister, she was a "tall, thin woman with dark hair, pale skin, and blood-red lips and nails" who was "*very* German." (Margaret Salinger, 71) At the time, it evidently did not bother the half-Jewish Salinger that Sylvia was "a low-level-official of the Nazi party" (Margaret Salinger, 71) whom he had arrested. His hatred of Nazis did not seem to be based on their political views but rather on the fact that they were trying to kill him and his comrades. He and Sylvia, according to Salinger, had a relationship that was "extremely intense, both physically and emotionally." (Margaret Salinger, 71) Their marriage probably took place in September or October 1945. By November, Salinger was honorably discharged from the army, but he signed a six month civilian contract with the Department of Defense. He and Sylvia lived in Gunzenhausen, Germany, until May, when they came to New York and moved in with his parents. A month later on June 13, 1946, Sylvia returned to Europe and then filed for divorce. They never saw each other again.

In later years, when he was disgusted with his second wife, Salinger would praise Sylvia to Claire as a "real woman who knew her own mind and had accomplished something at a young age." However, he also vilified her as "a terrible, dark woman of passion, an evil woman who bewitched him," calling her "Saliva." Salinger told his second wife that "Sylvia hated Jews as much as he hated Nazis." (Margaret Salinger, 71)

Writing for a Living

With his return to the United States, Salinger still feared he might lose his sanity. He continued living with his parents until 1947; spent his nights in Greenwich Village partying with a variety of girls, playing poker, hanging out at bars, and eating at his favorite restaurants; and threw himself into writing. In 1946, he nearly published a ninety-page novella about a boy named Holden Caulfield, but withdrew the work to revise it; however, his short story on Holden Caulfield, accepted in 1941, was finally published in the *New Yorker* in December 1946.

In January 1947, sick of big city life, he moved to a garage apartment in Tarrytown, New York. That same year, he sold two stories, one to *Mademoiselle* and one to *Cosmopolitan*. In the fall, he moved farther into the country to a barn studio in Stamford, Connecticut. Here he wrote one of his most famous stories, "A Perfect Day

Nation, and the *Atlantic Monthly* were not as impressed. Others, including *The United States Quarterly Book Review* and the *Catholic World,* complained about its use of profanity. (French, *Salinger*, 28) However, the public liked it; it was on the *New York Times* bestseller list for thirty weeks, reaching fourth place, its highest position, on October 21, 1951. (Alexander, 154) Salinger himself was upset with its success because people became interested in him as "the writer" and they expected him to give interviews and sign autographs, when he craved privacy.

On his return to the United States, Salinger rented an apartment in New York City, a place Claire, now a college student, referred to as the "black apartment" because everything in it was black or white—black sheets, black bookshelves, black coffee table. She felt it was a perfect reflection of his depression, for he fell into "black holes where he could hardly move, hardly talk." (Margaret Salinger, 75)

Claire and Salinger's romance did not progress smoothly, partly because Salinger's study of Eastern religions, in particular Zen Buddhism and Vedanta Hinduism, led him to believe that a man could not achieve true enlightenment if he sought worldly things, especially money and women, who are thought to be "phlegm, filth, and excreta." (Margaret Salinger, 86) Therefore, Salinger would sometimes disappear for months without saying a word to Claire.

On one of his absences, while he was traveling in Florida and Mexico in 1952, the Valley Forge Military Academy selected him for one of three Distinguished Alumni of the Year awards. Salinger, rather embarrassed over the publicity, was thankful he was out of the country so he did not have to attend the ceremony.

After the success of *Catcher,* Salinger published less. One of his stories was printed in 1952 and one in 1953, but none appeared in 1954.

This photograph of Salinger's home in Cornish, New Hampshire, was taken in August 1987. Two Doberman pinschers (not shown) protect the property against intruders.

Moving to Cornish, New Hampshire

Hating the adulation he received as a public figure, Salinger, much like Holden in *The Catcher in the Rye,* wanted to "build . . . a little cabin somewhere with the dough I made and live there for the rest of my life." (*Catcher,* 199) He began making his dream a reality at the end of 1952 when he and his sister Doris traveled in Vermont and New Hampshire, looking for a secluded place Salinger could purchase. He found it outside Cornish, New Hampshire, a small town across the river from Windsor, Vermont. High up in the hills, miles in the country, and accessible from a dirt road lay a dilapidated red cottage on ninety acres of land. The cottage nestled at the edge of a meadow with a huge drop-off to a brook below; beyond the brook lay a forest. Although the view was breathtaking, the cottage was a wreck. Doris was shocked when her brother bought the property because she considered the cottage uninhabitable, with no running water, no bathroom, a barnlike living room with squirrels living in the rafters, a tiny water-stained bedroom, a hovel for a kitchen, and a wobbly staircase leading to a small loft. (Margaret Salinger, 82) On his thirty-fourth birthday on January 1, 1953, Salinger turned his back on what many consider the American dream—wealth, national recognition, and public adulation—and moved into this dilapidated cottage in Cornish, happily cutting wood with his new chain saw and carrying buckets of water. (Skow, 15)

Marrying Claire

Wanting a soul mate, Salinger asked Claire Douglas to quit Radcliffe College, where she was enrolled, and come to Cornish to live with him. When she refused, Salinger vanished, leaving Claire totally devastated. Hospitalized for mononucleosis, she grew to appreciate a young Harvard graduate who visited her often, and that spring, she eloped with him. However, she was very unhappy, and within a year, their marriage was annulled.

While Claire lay hospitalized, *Nine Stories,* a collection of short stories that were previously printed in various magazines, was published on April 6, 1953. It rose to ninth place on the *New York Times* bestseller list, staying there for more than three months. (French, *Salinger*, 30)

Sometime in 1953, Salinger returned to Cornish, where he began palling around with some of the high school students, meeting them at a local eatery, going to their games, and entertaining them with record parties at his home. (Skow, 15) When Shirlie Blaney asked to interview him for what he thought was the school newspaper, Jerry, as she and the other high schoolers called Salinger, agreed. However, he was outraged when the article appeared on the editorial page of the *Claremont* (New Hampshire) *Daily Eagle* on November 13. Abruptly, he ended his friendship with the high schoolers. (Lundquist, 28–29; French, *Salinger*, 30)

In the summer of 1954, Salinger began courting Claire again. That fall, when he pressured her to live with him, she agreed, but she continued her studies at Radcliffe. After one semester, Salinger gave her an ultimatum—her degree or him. This time Claire chose him, immediately quitting school with only one semester left until graduation. Salinger, age thirty-six, and Claire, age twenty-one, were married on February 17, 1955. Salinger's story "Franny," which was published in the *New Yorker* on January 29, 1955, was a wedding gift to Claire, the model for Franny, who has Claire's manners, looks, and even her blue suitcase.

From the beginning, their marriage was not ideal. Claire was almost a prisoner in the red cottage in Cornish. She saw no one, for the Salingers kept their distance from their neighbors. She called no one, having severed all of her ties to the outside world when she left Radcliffe. At Salinger's request, she had burned all of her papers, left her friends, and never visited her family. Now she was alone with her critical husband, a man who often refused to talk to her, preferring to spend sixteen-hour days locked away by himself writing. Sometimes he worked all night and into the next day, and Claire was not allowed to disturb him except to bring him three meals daily, as he required. In November 1955, Salinger published his first long story about the Glass family, "Raise High the Roof Beam, Carpenters," in the *New Yorker.*

At the end of the year on December 10, 1955, Peggy was born. Having a baby in the house did not fit into

Salinger's schedule, and he immediately began building his own place a quarter mile into the forest. His cement, cinder block cabin (called the Green House) became his new writing place, and here he spent hours, sometimes days, pounding on his typewriter and searching for God, which were "inseparable disciplines" for him. (Ian Hamilton, 141) In spite of all the time and effort he spent on his work, he published nothing in 1956. It wasn't until May 4, 1957, that another story about the Glass family, "Zooey," appeared in the *New Yorker.*

Meanwhile, back at the Red House, Salinger's wife, who was suffering from severe depression following the birth of Peggy, struggled to care for the baby by herself. In winter 1957, she left her husband and found psychiatric help. Four months later, when Salinger came to ask her to come back to Cornish, she agreed to return. From this time on, Salinger allowed a few people to visit Claire. Several years later on February 13, 1960, their son, Matthew Robert, was born.

Throughout these early years of marriage, Salinger kept writing. But he established a better routine, so he was no longer writing sixteen hours a day. Now, he rose at dawn, worked until mid- or late morning, and spent the afternoons gardening, taking walks, playing with his children or dogs, and running errands. Peggy liked listening to the stories he made up for her and Matt. She found vacations with him wonderful, especially the frequent trips he took with his children to New York City, where they vacationed in first-class luxury at the Plaza Hotel and visited the zoo and the museums. (Margaret Salinger, 184–186) The entire family took winter vacations in Florida where they stayed in inexpensive hotels. Salinger also took time to doctor his children, spending hours researching his books on homeopathic medicine for a cure with natural substances instead of allowing them to visit a medical doctor. Sometimes he performed acupuncture, which the children dreaded because he jammed dowels, not needles, into their skins.

Seeking Religion

During these years, Salinger kept searching for religious enlightenment, following Zen Buddhism, Vedanta Hinduism, Scientology, Kriya yoga, Christian Science, the works of Edgar Cayce, macrobiotics, homeopathy, and acupuncture at various times. (Margaret Salinger, 95; Alsen, *Glass Stories,* 143) Claire thinks he switched religions, which she calls cults, because he was disappointed in his writings. She told her daughter that every time Jerry was nearly finished with a story, he would leave Cornish for weeks to go to New York or Montreal or Atlantic City to finish his work. But when he came back, his story was destroyed, and he had adopted a new "cult" with a "new super-encompassing God," which she had to follow rigidly. She believes he switched religions "to cover the fact that Jerry had just destroyed or junked or couldn't face the quality of, or couldn't face publishing, what he had created." (Margaret Salinger, 95) Peggy thinks that her father might have had a second reason to join cults: to find a "landsman." (Margaret Salinger, 97) No matter what the reason, Salinger has continued to embrace various cults throughout his life.

Publishing Final Works

Although he faithfully wrote, Salinger hardly ever published. It took him two years after "Zooey" to finally publish another story; "Seymour, An Introduction," the story of young Seymour Glass, appeared on June 6, 1959, in the *New Yorker*. In spite of his sparse output, reporters were enthralled by Salinger's seclusion and constantly pried into his personal life. In the 1960s, Salinger was annoyed with journalists from *Newsweek* and the *New York Post,* who interviewed his acquaintances, and with

Life's Ernest Havemann, who called "hello" over Salinger's fence until Claire came to tell him that no reporter could meet her husband. Worse yet was the *New York Times,* which hired detectives to pry into Salinger's past, causing an "unspeakably bitter experience" for the author. (Ian Hamilton, 176)

Part of the reason the press became so interested in the private author was that he twice joined two stories into books. *Franny and Zooey,* published on September 14, 1961, was an immediate success, sitting in first place on the *New York Times Book Review*'s bestseller list for six months. (French, *Salinger*, 32) A year and a half later, *Raise High the Roof Beam, Carpenters and Seymour: An Introduction* was released on January 28, 1963. Salinger published only one other work, "Hapworth 16, 1924," in the *New Yorker* on June 19, 1965.

Breaking Relationships

Claire and Salinger's marriage was always rocky. By summer 1966, Claire, distraught over her isolation, loveless marriage, and demanding spouse, became physically ill. Although she filed for divorce on September 9, she remained married to Salinger for another year. However, on the advice of her doctor, who felt that continuing her marriage would "seriously injure her health and endanger her reason," she finalized the divorce on October 3, 1967. (Alexander, 236) In the divorce settlement, Claire got almost everything, including the house, the land, the children, and child support.

In 1966, Salinger had purchased 475 adjoining acres on which he built a house for himself. The small one level ranch, with a living room, a galley kitchen, a guest bedroom for his children, a cellar, and Salinger's own bedroom, bath, and study, is the home he has lived in since then. For years, Salinger did his writing in his new study, which, Peggy says, housed several huge floor-to-ceiling safes containing his completed works. (Margaret Salinger, 307)

J. D. Salinger's son Matthew became an actor. Here he is shown in the 1991 film, *Captain America*.

A year after his divorce, Salinger, now forty-nine, took his children, ages twelve and eight, on a two-week trip to England and Scotland, where he met the teenage girl with whom he had been corresponding. Finding her unattractive, Salinger broke off the romance.

Salinger's relationship with his daughter also became strained. When Peggy, afraid of her thirty-four-year-old mother's college boyfriends (who seemed more interested in her than her mother), asked her father if she could move in with him, Salinger adamantly refused, telling her that she would interfere with his work. Thus, Peggy was sent to boarding school for eighth grade. By the time she was fifteen, she was rarely allowed to spend her vacations in Cornish, relying on friends to let her visit. A troubled teenager, Peggy starting having problems with the law and at school. She became pregnant and had an abortion, and also suffered from bulimia, but neither parent seems to have helped or guided her.

However, Salinger's relationship with his son was much better. Although Matthew was also sent to boarding school, he often came home on weekends, and his father spent time with him, even sitting in the rain and cold to watch football games at Dartmouth, something Salinger endured to make his son happy. He also took Matthew out for pizza, although he ate only organic food at home. After eating with his son, he returned home to vomit because he wished to rid his body of impure food. (Maynard, 144)

In the early 1970s, both of Salinger's parents died, but he seemed unaffected. Peggy says she was shocked and upset to receive a letter from her father informing her that his father had died some weeks earlier in spring 1970. He told her that he and Doris had arranged things with a "minimum of crap and ceremony." The next year, when his mother died, Salinger did not tell Peggy about her grandmother's death; she read about it in the newspaper. (Margaret Salinger, 338)

Meanwhile, Salinger wrote and wrote but never published. (Maynard, 158) *The Catcher in the Rye* continued to sell well, providing the writer with all the money he needed.

Living with Joyce Maynard

In September 1972, Joyce Maynard, a childlike-looking eighteen-year-old writer who had completed her first year at Yale, moved in with Salinger. They had met months earlier after Salinger wrote her a touching letter concerning her article in the *New York Times Magazine* on April 25, 1972. After the fifty-three-year-old recluse and the ambitious teenager corresponded during the summer, Joyce quit college and joined Salinger in Cornish.

Her descriptions of her life with him shed light on how Salinger lived after his divorce. Every morning he and Joyce ate unleavened bread and frozen peas (Salinger thought cooking removed the nutrients), meditated, did yoga, and wrote. In the afternoons, they took the ten-minute drive over dirt roads to the covered bridge in Windsor, Vermont, where he picked up the mail and bought newspapers. Returning home, they read the papers and made dinner, which usually consisted of bread, steamed fiddlehead ferns, apple slices, and sometimes popcorn. If they had meat, it was barely cooked organic ground lamb. Eating off folding metal TV trays, they watched television shows (Salinger always liked TV). Often, Salinger retired to his study to write letters; sometimes they read or watched old movies. (Maynard, 110–112, 156)

Although Maynard reported that Salinger wrote for hours daily and that he had finished at least two full-length manuscripts which he stored in a safe the size of a room, she never saw any of his writings. (Maynard, 106, 158)

Maynard says their love affair lasted seven months, until March 1973. When Salinger and Maynard, who was hoping to have a child with Salinger, were vacationing in

J. D. SALINGER STRUCK UP A CORRESPONDENCE WITH JOYCE MAYNARD AFTER HER ESSAY ON TEENAGE LIFE IN THE 1970S APPEARED IN THE *NEW YORK TIMES MAGAZINE*. MAYNARD AUCTIONED OFF THE LETTERS TWENTY YEARS LATER, LONG AFTER THEIR RELATIONSHIP BECAME HISTORY.

The New York Times Magazine

APRIL 23, 1972 SECTION 6

Daytona Beach with his children, Salinger, deciding he did not want any more children, told her to go back to Cornish and move out before he returned.

Protecting His Privacy

Since his retirement to Cornish, Salinger has vigorously defended his right to privacy. He became irate when he found out that a pirated edition of his stories, *The Complete Uncollected Short Stories of J. D. Salinger*, began circulating in 1974. Salinger's lawyers sued John Greenberg, who had put together stories Salinger had published in magazines between 1940 and 1948, for copyright violations. So upset was Salinger that he telephoned Lacey Fosburgh of the *New York Times* to complain that "some stories, my property, have been stolen." (quoted in Lutz, 39) He told Fosburgh that he disliked publishing intensely: "There is a marvelous peace in not publishing. It's peaceful. Publishing is a terrible invasion of my privacy. I like to write. I love to write. But I write just for myself and my own pleasure." (quoted in Beller, 145) The conversation helped make the author's life even less private, for it ended up as a front-page article in the *New York Times* on November 3, 1974. The lawsuit was settled in 1986 when the court ruled in Salinger's favor.

In 1980, Salinger became upset when he felt his privacy had been violated by Betty Eppes, a pretty, young Southern journalist whom he had agreed to meet for an interview. After talking with her briefly, he became angry when a local store owner approached him and asked to shake his hand. Feeling that this unwanted advance happened because of the interview, Salinger shouted at Eppes, "Don't call my home; don't call any of my friends. Just leave Windsor; leave Cornish, and leave me alone!" (quoted in Alexander, 267)

Salinger's biggest legal battle occurred when Ian Hamilton decided to write a biography of him. Although the author refused to visit with Hamilton, the biographer wrote *J. D.*

Salinger: A Writing Life. In 1986, before the book went to press, Salinger obtained a copy and was horrified to read quotes from his unpublished letters which he had written to family and friends between 1939 and 1961. Although Hamilton had legally obtained these letters, which are housed in university libraries and open for public inspection, Salinger sued Hamilton and Random House, the publisher, for infringements of copyright and invasions of privacy. In November 1986, the judge ruled in favor of Hamilton, but Salinger immediately appealed the decision. The Federal Appeals Court ruled in favor of Salinger in 1987, and Ian Hamilton was blocked from publishing the biography. After taking out all of the quotes from Salinger's letters, Hamilton published a book called *In Search of J. D. Salinger*.

Pursuing Romance

Although Salinger was busy in the 1970s and 1980s writing for his own pleasure and barring publications which invaded his privacy, he still had time to pursue romantic liaisons. When she was conducting research for her book of memoirs, Maynard learned that she was only one of a series of young women who corresponded and later lived with Salinger after his divorce from Claire. Salinger's neighbor, Dan, told her, "There were always girls in one way or another. There's a woman living with him now. She's been around a few years. Before that, others came and went." (Maynard, 339) Dan told her that Salinger was picky about his girlfriends, rejecting both a young British girl he had flown to England to meet and a beautiful, intelligent college girl from California, who, in 1977 or 1978, had come to Windsor after exchanging letters with Salinger. (Maynard, 339–340)

One woman who particularly fascinated Salinger after Joyce Maynard was the actress Elaine Joyce. In 1981, the sixty-two-year-old writer watched the thirty-six-year-old actress perform on a sitcom. Just as he had with Claire,

Joyce Maynard, and the British and California girls, he wrote her a letter, and thus began a romantic relationship. The reclusive Salinger even traveled to Jacksonville, Florida, where the actress was appearing in a play. Elaine Joyce says their romance lasted through the middle 1980s. (Alexander, 273–274)

While he was dating Elaine Joyce, Salinger was also writing to Colleen O'Neill, a pretty, slim, serious girl who was almost a half century younger than him. (Margaret Salinger, 414) The two began corresponding in 1977 or 1978 after meeting on a bus ride when Colleen was on her way to Dartmouth. (Maynard, 327) In the summer of 1980, she worked as an *au pair*, but that fall, she gave up a college scholarship to marry a man named Mike whose young son she adopted. Mike described her as the "sweetest, most innocent girl" with "high values" who (like Sylvia, Claire, and Joyce Maynard) "wanted so badly to make something of herself." (Maynard, 329) After her marriage, Colleen openly continued her correspondence with Salinger, which Mike thought was harmless, but on Thanksgiving Day in 1983, she abruptly left her husband and son and later went to live with Salinger in Cornish. Several years after that, when she was making her yearly visit to their son, her ex-husband noticed she was wearing a wedding band. Colleen had become the third Mrs. Jerome David Salinger.

Trying to Stay Out of the Public Eye

With the passing years, Salinger has more aggressively tried to protect his privacy from the media. In 1988, he became furious with two freelance paparazzi, who, after stalking him for days, blocked his car at a supermarket. The author crashed his grocery cart into one and tried to punch the other with his fist. Unfortunately, the two managed to take a most unflattering portrait of him looking like an old, angry man ready to hit the camera. They published it in the *New York Post* in April. (Alexander, 288–289)

His relationship with Colleen became public knowledge in October 1992 when there was a fire at the Salinger home that destroyed about one-half of the house. The fire was reported by a woman who identified herself as "Mrs. Salinger." CNN and major newspapers picked up the story immediately. (Lutz, 42)

Salinger even rebuffed people he knew. His former housekeeper warned biographer Paul Alexander in the 1990s "to be careful of him because he really gets angry," glaring with his "big beady black eyes." (Alexander, 295) She told him of the frightening experience she and her mother had when they went to his home for a cancer fundraising drive. He stopped them in the driveway with a gun in his hands, ordering them to "Just go away." Even though he gave a donation, he warned them, "Don't ever come back again." (Alexander, 295)

In 1997, amazon.com announced a new publication of *Hapworth 16, 1924*, which renewed national interest in the recluse. After a *New York Times* critic wrote a negative review of the story, originally published in 1965. Salinger changed his mind, and Orchises Press announced that the book publication was put on hold indefinitely. (Alexander, 295–299)

Salinger made one more attempt to protect his privacy legally. In 1998, he discovered that a movie being shown at the Iranian film festival at Lincoln Center in New York City—Dariush Mehrjui's *Pari,* made in 1995—was an unauthorized adaptation of *Franny and Zooey*. When Salinger's attorney threatened legal action, the film society cancelled the screenings.

Although he was successful in winning legal battles and driving off journalists to protect his privacy, Salinger could not stop Joyce Maynard from publishing her memoirs of their love affair; *At Home in the World: A Memoir* came out in 1998. Nor could he keep his daughter from publishing her revealing account of her life with her father in *Dream*

Catcher: A Memoir, printed in 2000. Both of these books have shed great insight on the life, habits, and thoughts of the reclusive, private man.

Living in the Twilight Years

In his elderly years, Salinger does not have many close relationships, even with his family. Matt Salinger continues to have a good connection with his father, and he seems to have inherited his father's acting talents. Salinger encouraged his son to become an actor and proudly attended his off-Broadway productions in the 1980s. (French, *Revisited,* 14)

However, Salinger's relationship with his daughter became worse as she grew older. According to Peggy, he did not want to interrupt his work and be inconvenienced with any of her problems, including her attempted suicide in December 1984, and her suffering from the Epstein-Barr virus, which left her incapacitated and unable to hold a job. (Margaret Salinger, 396–403, 416) Their relationship hit a new low when she was hospitalized with complications from pregnancy in 1993, and he told her to abort her baby.

Even Salinger's sister, who once adored him, has come to see him as a very flawed person. When he refused to take time to visit or help her after her heart attack in the 1990s, she told her niece, "I love him . . . but I have to admit that he's a b------d . . . anything that interferes with him, with his work, is dismissed. . . . [Furthermore,] he takes any opportunity to dig the knife in." (Margaret Salinger, 428)

Salinger continues to live as a recluse in Cornish, New Hampshire, with his younger wife. He continues to protect his privacy hawkishly, granting no interviews, discouraging uninvited callers, living off the publications of four books, and publishing nothing new. It's possible that Salinger still occupies his time by writing, although that seems doubtful since Peggy reported that in the late 1990s her father's old study/bedroom, which held his safes, was converted into a sewing room for Colleen, an avid quilter who wins prizes at the local fair in Cornish. (Margaret Salinger, 414) Peggy did not mention what has happened to the safes with the unpublished manuscripts.

Salinger has, as his daughter says, “spent his life busy writing his heart out,” but in so doing, he has lived an unbalanced life. (Margaret Salinger, 429) Peggy’s judgment of her father and his work is probably accurate: “It seems to me that some very badly behaved, morally bankrupt, nasty, egotistical people have created some very beautiful art.” (Margaret Salinger, 423)

Chapter 2

Salinger's Times

Jerome David Salinger was born a few weeks after World War I ended on November 11, 1918. He published most of his works as a young man, just before and after World War II, in the late 1940s and early 1950s. His last story appeared in 1965.

The Precarious Twenties

Salinger grew up in a decade known as both "The Roaring Twenties" and "The Jazz Age" that brought great changes in American life. The country grew economically, and the people cast off old attitudes and lifestyles.

New Ways of Life

America became an urban nation in the 1920s as people moved from farms to the cities. Overall, the American economy flourished, with businesses thriving and new technology developing. However, the newfound wealth was unbalanced. While a number of businessmen, such as Sol Salinger, grew rich, laborers and farmers became poorer, many losing their land and becoming sharecroppers.

For prosperous Americans the 1920s was a wonderful decade. Because of Henry Ford almost every American family could afford a car, which allowed people new ways to get to work, see distant places, or merely have fun. Other scientific advances also contributed to the

THIS CARTOON DEPICTS A WOMAN ON A BALLOT BOX IN VICTORY AFTER THE PASSAGE OF THE NINETEETH AMENDMENT TO THE CONSTITUTION GAVE WOMEN THE RIGHT TO VOTE.

well-being of Americans. Millions of families had new household appliances, such as electric refrigerators, electric washing machines, and vacuum cleaners. (Freidel, 260) Homes were equipped with radios, which blared the world news and provided entertainment, and telephones, which gave Americans quick access to just about any person. As chemists, biologists, and bacteriologists improved public health and lengthened the average life span, death rates from typhoid, tuberculosis, diphtheria, and scarlet fever were reduced. (Dulles, 348–349)

Women began playing more powerful roles in society. They were given the right to vote with the passage of the Nineteenth Amendment to the Constitution on August 26,

THE ADVENT OF TELEVISION AS A STAPLE IN ORDINARY PEOPLE'S HOMES IN THE 1950S CHANGED LIFE IN AMERICA MORE THAN ALL OF POSTWAR LITERATURE.

1920. Freed from some of their time-consuming household chores because of the new inventions, more women began to work outside the home.

Younger people embraced relaxed moral codes. Young women painted their lips a deep red and dressed in short skirts, rolled-down silk stockings, and short "bobbed" hair. "Flappers" and their "beaus" loved going to "speakeasies," nightclubs where they illegally drank liquor (the Prohibition Amendment, which banned the sale of alcoholic beverages in the United States, was ratified in January 1919), listened to the new jazz music made popular by "Jelly Roll" Morton, Louis Armstrong, and Bessie Smith, and danced the modern Charleston. Here, they could talk about their heroes—famous movie stars, baseball's Babe Ruth, and the greatest of them all, aviator Charles Lindbergh, who flew solo across the Atlantic in 1927.

Smoldering beneath the seemingly placid surface were rivalries and social tensions. (Snowman, 34) Juvenile delinquency and crime rose steadily as gangs formed, in part because people started to buy liquor from underworld sources. Widespread prejudice and public intolerance were also marks of this decade. Any nonwhite, non-Anglo-Saxon, non-Protestant was targeted, including Jewish Americans, such as the Salingers. "Outsiders"—African Americans, Jews, Roman Catholics, foreigners, and political radicals—were held responsible for all modern problems.

Literature and the Arts

New writers expressed great disillusionment with this new age, referring to themselves as the "lost generation." Finding American life totally unsatisfying, some, such as T. S. Eliot, Ernest Hemingway, and F. Scott Fitzgerald, fled abroad. Fitzgerald, author of *The Great Gatsby* (1925), criticized the affluent Americans whose idealistic dreams had given way to cynical pleasure-seeking. Playwright Eugene O'Neill, the father of Salinger's first love interest, Oona, dominated the dramatic theater scene with *The Emperor Jones* (1920), *Anna Christie* (1922), and *The Hairy Ape* (1922).

An estimated 50 million to 100 million people, including young Salinger, crowded into the theaters to watch silent films with stars such as comedian Charlie Chaplin, who later married Oona O'Neill. Movie theaters became even more popular with the introduction of talking films in 1927. (Freidel, 260; Dulles, 346–347)

Magazines also reflected the era. Of greatest importance were the conservative *Saturday Evening Post* and *Readers' Digest,* and the sophisticated *New Yorker*, founded in 1925, Salinger's top choice. (Freidel, 262)

The Crash

As the decade drew to a close, more and more optimistic Americans invested in the stocks of corporations, causing stock values to soar even though the prices could not be justified. Finally, the good times came to a sudden end with the stock market crash in 1929.

The Great Depression of the Thirties

For more than ten years, Americans endured the Great Depression. However, not everyone was affected by the poor economy, including Salinger's father, who prospered during this decade.

Hard Times

After the stock market crash, America's economy suffered, as banks stopped loaning money to businesses, businesses cut production, and people lost their jobs. With little money, Americans quit buying goods, and factories and stores closed, causing more unemployment. Banks failed, and people lost their life savings. Farm products were not purchased, and farmers were forced to desert their farms. Then, in 1934, a devastatingly dry summer changed much of the land in the Southwest and Midwest into dust, further destroying the struggling farmers, a plight vividly described by John Steinbeck in *The Grapes of Wrath.*

Staying alive was hard work for many people. Bread lines and soup kitchens were set up by charities to keep people from starving. Multiple families crowded together in small apartments, while homeless people built tin shacks in vacant areas called Hoovervilles, a derisive term referring to Herbert Hoover, who was president when the Great Depression began. (Snowman, 45–46)

Americans eagerly looked forward to The New Deal promised by Franklin Delano Roosevelt, elected president in 1932. His threefold program consisted of relief (feeding and housing the unemployed), recovery (restoring the nation's economy), and reform (establishing permanent measures to help particular aspects of society). (Snowman, 61–62)

Literature and the Arts

The arts flourished throughout the decade. Thornton Wilder, author of the play *Our Town* (1938), and Eugene O'Neill were the major playwrights. Some novelists, like William Faulkner, whose *The Sound and the Fury* (1929) brought him national acclaim, seemed untouched by the Depression, while others, such as Ernest Hemingway, Thomas Wolfe, and John Steinbeck, produced works of social criticism. Two female writers also achieved fame: Margaret Mitchell, author of the bestseller *Gone With the Wind* (1936), and Pearl S. Buck, the 1938 Nobel Prize winner for *The Good Earth* (1931).

World Crisis

The Depression was not limited to the United States. Worldwide suffering helped bring about the rise of ruthless, powerful dictators, including Adolf Hitler in Germany, and military leaders in Japan, who promised to reestablish a strong economy. Once in power, Hitler and the Japanese rulers began to take control of neighboring countries, actions which finally led to World War II. In the United States, the Depression lasted until World War II, when military spending stimulated the economy.

World War II

Throughout the 1920s and 1930s, the United States had successfully stayed out of alliances with other countries, but this changed in the early 1940s. Americans watched as Hitler's Nazis overran Poland on September 1, 1939, and as France, Great Britain, and other countries (called the Allies) declared war on Germany, and later on Italy and Japan, Germany's Axis partners. Two years later, America was swept into the war after the Japanese attacked Pearl Harbor on December 7, 1941, killing many Americans. A few days later, Germany and Italy also declared war on the United States.

The Battles

Angry with the unjust attack, the Americans dedicated themselves to the war effort. Fifteen million American men served in the armed forces, many of them, such as Salinger, volunteering for duty. To commence a western assault on the Nazis, the American and British forces landed in Normandy, France, on D-day, June 6, 1944. Five Allied divisions, including Sergeant Salinger's, were put on shore despite high winds and rough seas. With no natural harbor for the Allies to land supplies, they pushed north to the port of Cherbourg, capturing it on June 27. The intense battle for the rest of Normandy was made worse by terrain interwoven with hedgerows and deep ditches where Germans waited in ambush. In spite of great losses, the Allied troops advanced to Paris, liberating it on August 25. From here, they swept through France, Belgium, and the Netherlands, driving the Germans back. In a desperate attempt to gain a port, the Germans attacked in what became known as the Battle of the Bulge, but they were repelled by the Allies and forced to retreat. Germany surrendered on May 7, 1945.

When Japan kept on fighting, America's new president, Harry S. Truman, ordered the use of the atomic bomb, hitting Hiroshima, Japan, on August 6, 1945, and Nagasaki three days later. Japan surrendered on September 2, 1945, and the war was finally over.

The Home Front

Those who remained in the United States worked hard to help win the war. Factories were converted into plants for war supplies, and with the men away fighting, thousands of women began working in them.

The war led to other advances in science besides the atomic bomb, including new or improved jet airplanes, helicopters, radar, and guided missiles. Technicians worked on providing edible food for soldiers, which led to precooked frozen foods. These became available to all consumers after the war. Scientists researched drugs, trying to find ways to help the wounded and save lives, resulting in the wonder drugs sulfapyradine and penicillin, and other antibiotics that controlled tuberculosis, kidney infections, and other diseases. (Davis and Lunger, 6–7)

Literature and the Arts

Not very much literature of lasting merit was published during the war, although classics, such as *Oklahoma!,* by Richard Rodgers and Oscar Hammerstein, and *The Glass Menagerie,* by Tennessee Williams, appeared on stage. (Snowman, 113) J. D. Salinger started his publishing career in the 1940s, selling stories to national magazines.

The Postwar Forties and the Prosperous Fifties

Americans prospered economically in the next decade and a half, but the years were marked with tension. Although the United Nations, founded on October 24, 1945, was meant to help provide world security, the opposing political ideologies of democracy and communism struggled for supremacy.

The Cold War

The United States and the Soviet Union, which had fought on the same side in World War II, became bitter enemies following the war. The Soviet Union, a totalitarian state opposed to democracy, helped the communists seize control of most of the countries in Eastern Europe and China, while the United States, the world's greatest democracy, became the defender of non-communist nations threatened by the communists. The struggle between the American-led democracy and the communist nations became known as the Cold War.

The Korean War started when communist North Korea, backed by the Soviet Union, invaded South Korea on June 25, 1950. Dwight D. Eisenhower, elected president in 1952, worked out a ceasefire on July 27, 1953, but no one was able to claim victory.

Americans' fears of communism were fueled by Senator Joseph McCarthy, who began a type of witch hunt to find and eliminate Communists who had infiltrated America.

With spectacular, unsupported accusations, McCarthy tried to weed out enemies to America, giving birth to McCarthyism in early 1950. It was not until late 1954 that the Senate stopped McCarthy, and investigations into subversive activities and peoples were conducted more logically.

As the Cold War escalated, the two superpowers began building nuclear weapons, threatening the use of force, engaging in propaganda, and aiding weak nations. They also participated in a missile development race. Convinced they were ahead, Americans were shocked when the Russians launched the first successful satellite into space in October 1957.

Life in America

Meanwhile, Americans were readjusting to peacetime life. The American economy was thriving. Factories and businesses were booming. And the nation's wealth was enjoyed by more and more people as labor unions became strong, gaining high wages and good benefits for their members. Many of the women who had worked in factories during the war gladly gave up their paychecks and were content to stay home to raise their families, but those who remained in the workforce often found widespread discrimination with unequal pay and few opportunities for promotion.

The young adults who had grown up in the privation of the 1930s and participated in the horrendous war of the early 1940s were now ready to embrace a good life. They started families, producing a generation of babies that would later be known as the baby boomers, and they built nice homes on the fringes of the cities, starting suburban living.

Literature and the Arts

In postwar America many authors, including Salinger, were disillusioned with American life. The antihero—a failure, rebel, or victim—became standard in American fiction, beginning with Arthur Miller's *Death of a Salesman* in 1949. In 1951, Salinger's *The Catcher in the Rye* portrayed the dilemma of a young nonconformist hero longing for a meaningful life. Other Jewish-American writers—Saul Bellow, Bernard Malamud, and Philip Roth—wrote about Jewish heroes who did not fit into American society. Black writers, such as Ralph Ellison and James Baldwin, reflected on the plight of black Americans. Southern short-story writers, including Eudora Welty, Flannery O'Connor, and Carson McCullers, examined changes in the South. Other popular writers, such as Norman Mailer and John Updike, looked at lonely, disappointed Americans, and Allen Ginsberg's "beat" poetry was a plea for the individual to rise up against conformity.

Television became a fixture in many American homes. No longer were people spending most of their leisure hours reading, going to movies, or listening to the radio. Now Americans, including Salinger, clicked on the TV.

A new style of music called rock 'n' roll became popular with teenagers in the mid-1950s. Elvis Presley not only sang and strummed, but also swiveled his hips, leaving adolescents begging for more. (Davis and Lunger, 100)

The Turbulent Sixties

The decade of the sixties continued the trends following World War II.

Foreign Affairs and the Vietnam War

In foreign affairs, the United States continued the Cold War with the Soviet Union. When Soviet ships brought equipment to install nuclear missile-launching sites in Fidel Castro's Cuba, President John F. Kennedy ordered a blockade on October 22, 1962, to stop further shipments of arms; the missile crisis and a nuclear war were avoided when the Soviet ships turned around.

However, it was the Vietnam War—which began in 1954 with the battle of Dien Bien Phu as Communists and non-Communists struggled to control South Vietnam—that proved to be the biggest quagmire of the 1960s. Hundreds of

PROTESTS IN WASHINGTON, D.C., AGAINST THE VIETNAM WAR BECAME COMMONPLACE IN THE LATE 1960S.

thousands of American troops were drafted to fight. However, unlike World War II, many Americans bitterly opposed this war, staging antiwar demonstrations and causing President Lyndon B. Johnson not to seek reelection. In 1968, Richard Nixon was chosen to lead the country.

Life in America

At home the economy expanded and more people were able to leave the crowded cities to enjoy life in the suburbs. However, poverty was a problem in the cities, and violent crimes, although especially bad in the inner cities, also spread to the suburbs.

The Civil Rights Movement of the 1960s was the main domestic social issue. Staging demonstrations, African Americans, under the leadership of Dr. Martin Luther King Jr., attempted to make their plight known to the American people. The Civil Rights Act of 1964 legally eliminated discrimination in employment, voter registration, and public housing, while the Civil Rights Act of 1968 ended discrimination in the selling and renting of housing. Besides African Americans, other disenfranchised people, such as American Indians, Mexican Americans, and women, also began advocating for greater rights.

The assassinations of three prominent Americans sent the nation into mourning. First was the murder of President John F. Kennedy on November 22, 1963, who was shot as he traveled by motorcade through Dallas, Texas. The second took place in Memphis, Tennessee, on April 4, 1969, when Martin Luther King Jr. was assassinated as he stood on the balcony of a motel. With the death of the champion of nonviolent civil rights protests, some African Americans chose to engage in more violent methods to gain their rights. Senator Robert F. Kennedy's death followed soon after; he was gunned down while campaigning for the presidential nomination in Los Angeles on June 4, 1968.

Science, Literature, and the Arts

Along with cultural unrest, scientific and technological advancements continued, and the exploration of outer space became a reality. On May 5, 1961, astronaut Alan B. Shepard Jr. became the first American to travel in space. Eight years later, on July 20, 1969, Neil A. Armstrong set his feet on the moon.

Television continued to gain popularity, while the film industry began showing movies at outdoor drive-in theaters, an attraction for families and teenagers.

Probably the greatest impact on the arts in this decade was the new rock group that came from Liverpool, England. The Beatles became the most popular singers in rock music history. Literary artists of the 1960s continued writing about lonely, disillusioned people. Many of the earlier writers continued to produce popular works, and women such as Alice Walker, Joyce Carol Oates, and Sylvia Plath became prominent.

Although Salinger is still alive, he quit publishing in the mid-1960s. Later decades, therefore, have had no effect on his published works.

The Catcher in the Rye

J. D. SALINGER

THE CATCHER IN THE RYE IS J. D. SALINGER'S ONLY PUBLISHED NOVEL. IT CONTINUES TO BE BANNED FROM SCHOOL LIBRARIES MORE THAN FIFTY YEARS LATER—AND TO BE WIDELY READ.

Chapter 3

The Catcher in the Rye

THE CATCHER IN THE RYE, Salinger's only published novel, was published on July 16, 1951. It is the story of an upper-middle-class, urban, sixteen-year-old male who in 1949 or 1950 journeys to New York after being expelled from school, and participates in a chaotic, bleak adult world. Holden Caulfield relates forty-eight hours in his life, describing his pessimistic attitudes about society and the world as he thinks about sex, adults, and American values.

Plot

Telling his story while he is in southern California in a mental hospital or sanitarium recovering from a nervous breakdown, Holden Caulfield flashes back to his final days at Pencey Prep, an elite private high school in Pennsylvania, just before Christmas the previous December.

Holden has been expelled from Pencey, but is still at school because his parents do not expect him home in Manhattan until Wednesday. On his last Saturday, he says good-bye to his history teacher, Mr. Spencer, who annoys Holden by lecturing him about his lack of motivation and poor scholarship, advising him on how he must understand that "life is a game" and that he needs to "play it according to the rules." (8)

Returning to his dorm room, Holden becomes annoyed with his irritating neighbor, Robert Ackley, and gets upset when he learns that his roommate, Ward Stradlater, has a date with Jane Gallagher, an old friend of Holden's. Adding to his distress, Stradlater harshly criticizes the English composition he asked Holden to write for him. Holden loses the ensuing physical fight, packs his bags, and goes to Manhattan.

On the train ride to the city he meets the mother of a Pencey classmate whom he considers "the biggest b------d that ever went to Pencey" (54), but he makes up stories about how well-liked he is as school. Once in New York City, he registers at the Edmont Hotel and calls Faith Cavendish, a woman he has never met but whom he thinks will have sex with him because she is a former stripper. However, she will not meet him. He then flirts with three women from Seattle in the hotel lounge, but ends up alone with the bill. His trip to Ernie's Nightclub in Greenwich Village is fruitless, for he leaves almost immediately when he sees one of his brother's former girlfriends, Lillian Simmons. When Holden returns to the hotel, Maurice, the elevator man, arranges a visit for him from a prostitute, Sunny. Holden, too scared and too depressed to go through with it, pays her to leave, but she returns with Maurice and demands more money. When Holden refuses to pay, Maurice punches him in the stomach, and Sunny steals the money.

After sleeping a few hours, Holden calls Sally Hayes, a girl he has dated in the past, and arranges to go to a play with her that afternoon. To avoid Maurice, he checks his bags at Grand Central Station, where he eats a late breakfast and enjoys talking with two nuns about *Romeo and Juliet.* Hoping to see his ten-year-old sister, Phoebe, he goes to Central Park. Here he is cheered by a young boy singing, "If a body catch a body coming through the rye." (115)

His date with Sally does not go as well as he hoped. At lunch, Holden talks to Sally about his disillusionment with life and suggests that they run off to New England and live in a cabin in the woods. Their date ends when realistic Sally dismisses this idea, and Holden calls her a "royal pain in the ass." (133)

After meeting his student advisor from a previous school, Carl Luce, at a bar and then getting drunk, Holden wanders around Central Park. He becomes more and more concerned about the ducks in the lagoon, breaks a record he bought for Phoebe, and finally sneaks into his family's apartment to see his sister. He tells her that he has decided that his mission in life is to be a "catcher in the rye," a person standing at the edge of a cliff, ready to catch the little children playing in a rye field when they get too close to the edge. When his parents return home, Holden goes to spend the night at the home of his former English teacher, Mr. Antolini. After listening to his former teacher lecture him about how he is headed for a serious fall, Holden finally falls asleep but awakens startled when Mr. Antolini pats his head. Afraid that Antolini is making sexual advances toward him, he quickly leaves and spends the rest of the night at Grand Central Station.

The next day, Holden asks Phoebe to meet him because he wants to tell her good-bye before he heads out west, where he plans to live as a "deaf-mute." As he is waiting for her, he becomes more upset and delusional, believing that every time he crosses the street he will disappear. In his idealism of being a "catcher in the rye," Holden becomes "near crazy" when he sees "f--- you" written on the walls of Phoebe's school and the Natural History Museum. (201, 202) After he meets his sister, he gives up his plan of heading west when she insists on going with him. Later they go to Central Park, and Holden happily watches Phoebe ride the carousel (*Note: Salinger spells it "carrousel," but the correct spelling is used here*), reaching for the gold ring.

In the last chapter, Holden, in California at a mental institution where his brother, D. B., often visits him, confides that writing his story has made him miss people, even the "jerks." Cautiously optimistic, he plans to go to a new school in the fall.

Pennsylvania Station was one of the many Manhattan landmarks that figured in Holden Caulfield's world.

Themes and Issues

The Catcher in the Rye is a dark coming-of-age novel, a type of literature that features a young protagonist who begins in confusion, moves toward maturity, usually overcomes obstacles, and ultimately triumphs. Holden begins in the typical manner as an unhappy teenager who questions how to live in a false world. By the end of the novel, he receives some insight as he realizes that children need to grow up and take risks even if they might get hurt. But, unlike most coming-of-age novels, his epiphany does not cause him to triumph. Instead, he has a nervous breakdown and is sent to a mental hospital in California.

The Phony World

"Phony" is Holden's word to describe anything superficial, shallow, or insincere. He encounters phony people with false values everywhere he goes—D. B., Elkton Hill's headmaster (Mr. Haas), Mr. Spencer, Stradlater, Sally Hayes,

Ernie, Carl Luce. All of them have "an endless appetite for the glamour of appearance, for the vanity of effect and approval." (Rowe, 84) Therefore, he denounces his brother D. B., who was once a "terrific" short-story writer but has become a "prostitute" by seeking riches and fame in Hollywood. He despises his old Elkton Hills headmaster, Mr. Haas, who is charming to the "best" parents but pays no attention to "fat or corny-looking" ones. (14) And he disapproves of Ernie, the piano player at the nightclub who sacrificed true artistry for audience approval by showing off with a mirror focused on his face.

According to Holden, shallow, superficial people have created a world in which phoniness abounds. Broadway plays are "artificial, phony, and nearly always wrongly appreciated." (Pinsker, 74) The Christmas pageant at Radio City Music Hall is so nonreligious that "old Jesus probably would've puked if He [had] seen it." (137) Falsely sentimental Hollywood movies bring out the phoniness in people, such as the woman at Radio City who sobs during the picture but has no real compassion, refusing to take her child to the bathroom. (139) Books and magazine fiction feature the same types of heroes, "lean-jawed guys named David," and heroines, "phony girls named Linda or Marcia." (53) The bars are meccas for "shallow supersophisticates or self-satisfied intellectuals" (Galloway, 31) like Lillian Simmons and Carl Luce.

The few who act with sincerity and authenticity, Holden appreciates and praises. Thus, he is uplifted when he sees a six-year-old boy innocently singing, "If a body catch a body coming through the rye," (115) and he approves of Estelle Fletcher, the black woman who earnestly sings "Little Shirley Beans," the recording he purchases for Phoebe.

Although readers and critics have pointed out that Holden, with his constant lies, pretenses, and insincerities, is himself a phony, critic Sanford Pinsker disagrees, claiming that Holden lies for different reasons than corrupt phonies. His lies are told for three reasons: to spare another's feelings, such as when he tells Mr. Spencer he has to get his equipment at the gym instead of saying he is sick of his teacher's browbeating; to avoid the bad aspects of life, such as when he says he has to get his bags when he thinks Mr. Antolini is making sexual advances toward him; and to give himself a chance to talk about loneliness and death, two topics of vital interest to him, such as when he converses with Mrs. Morrow, the mother of a student at Pencey Prep. (39) Holden's lies, therefore, do not make him superficial like others he sees.

Preservation of Innocence

The conflict that Holden sees between the real and the superficial worlds helps define his attitude about innocence, for he feels he needs to protect authentic children from the artificial adult world. The title of the book makes it clear that trying to preserve innocence is a primary theme in the novel. Holden sees innocence as the carefree world of young children happily playing in a field of rye, unaware that they are near the edge of a cliff. But as their "catcher in the rye," he stands there, ready to catch them before they fall off. Innocence, thus, is related to childhood and is antithetical to growing up.

Everyone Holden esteems is either an innocent or a protector of the innocents. Two girls, Jane Gallagher, his sweet childhood girlfriend, and Phoebe, his ten-year-old sister, are the major representatives of innocence. Holden, fearing that Jane, now a young woman, may be in danger of losing her innocence if she is seduced by Stradlater, physically attacks his roommate. Unlike Jane, Phoebe, who has not grown up, is the perfect example of innocence and goodness. Other than some adults Holden meets by chance, such as the nuns, only one meets with his approval. Until Mr. Antolini pats Holden's forehead, Holden sees him as a protector of the innocents. He showed compassion when a student at Elkton Hills, James Castle, committed suicide, and he befriends Holden, even welcoming him into his home in the middle of the night.

Since Holden sees nothing to admire in the superficial, hypocritical adult world, he resists growing up. As his thoughts about the statues of Indians and Eskimos at the Museum of Natural History demonstrates, he wants things to remain the same. At the end of the novel, Holden's attitude about not maturing seems to change as he looks at Phoebe riding on the carousel, trying to grab the gold ring, and he decides that, even though life is dangerous, children must be allowed to take risks and grow up.

Death

Critic Jane Mendelsohn accurately points out that *The Catcher in the Rye* is "a book about a *suicidal* smart-funny-preppy New York teenager. It [is] *all about death.*" (181) Holden, afraid he will die either physically or emotionally in the phony world in which he exists, often thinks about death. The novel strikes the keynote of death from the opening pages as Holden repeatedly uses death terminology: he says D. B.'s story, "The Secret Goldfish," "killed me;" if Pencey lost the football game, Holden explains, people "were supposed to commit suicide or something;" (2) after flunking four subjects, Holden relates, "I got the ax;" (4) Mrs. Spencer greets Holden with, "Are you frozen to death?"; (5) and Mr. Spencer reads Holden his paper on Egyptians who "wrapped up dead people." (11)

Holden's allusions to death continue throughout the novel. For example, he uses "kill" repeatedly. Sometimes the word refers to something he likes, such as when he refers to how Phoebe put the broken record pieces in her night table, and he says, "She kills me." (164) Other times he uses the word to show extreme anger, as when he fights with Stradlater, saying, "I'd've killed him." (43) Additional references to death are found when Sally refuses to go to a cabin in New England with Holden because they would "starve to death," (132) and Phoebe tells her brother that "Daddy'll kill you" (165, 166, 173) because he flunked out of school.

Besides using the motif of death, Holden thinks about death. He reminisces about two dead boys: classmate James Castle, who committed suicide by jumping out a window, and his brother Allie, who died from leukemia several years earlier. Holden idealizes Allie for his intelligence and sensitivity, and his death was one of the most traumatic experiences of Holden's life. Throughout the novel Holden is troubled when he remembers Allie's death. Reflecting on Allie's death leads Holden to also consider the possible death of the ducks in Central Park, wondering what happens to them when the lagoon freezes over.

Holden's most pressing concern with death is his own. At the beginning of the novel, as he is running across the road to Mr. Spencer's house, he says, "I felt like I was sort of disappearing." (5) Much later, his fear becomes more intense. After getting roughed up by Maurice, he declares, "I thought I was dying." (103) When Maurice and Sunny rob him, he confesses that he "felt like . . . committing suicide. [He] felt like jumping out the window." (104) But his worst fear of dying comes as he is walking down Fifth Avenue. Each time Holden gets to a curb he fears he will "just go down, down, down, and nobody'd ever see [him] again." (197) To save himself he calls on his dead brother to help him.

Fear of death, which brings change and destruction, remains a primary concern of Holden's throughout the novel.

Isolation and Loneliness

Holden never seems to fit into the world. During the time he is writing his story, he is out of the mainstream of life, confined to a mental hospital in California. Separated from his sister, his parents, his classmates, and his teachers, he is about as physically alone as a person can get.

This bodily separation is reinforced throughout the novel. It is seen at the hotels and nightclubs of New York.

HOLDEN CAULFIELD, IN HIS ISOLATION, CONTEMPLATED SUICIDE AFTER HE FLED HIS PREP SCHOOL AND CHECKED INTO A HOTEL IN NEW YORK.

For example, when almost everyone at Pencey Prep is at the football game, Holden is on Thomsen Hill by himself. When Stradlater is out on a date with his friend Jane, Holden sits in the empty dorm room writing an essay for him. He travels to New York alone, checks into a hotel alone, goes to the lounge alone, walks to Central Park alone, gets drunk alone. Even though he reaches out for company, he is constantly deserted and left by himself.

But the physical separation is not as bad as his emotional isolation. Since he believes he is different from others his age—being more moral, having a critical and creative mind, possessing a lively imagination, and desiring meaningful human contact and love (Bungert, 178)—Holden is an extremely lonely teenager. Searching for human companionship, he darts from one person to another, finding almost all human contact meaningless. Part of his isolation is his own fault, for he often holds himself aloof from others. For example, even though he wants love, he is too afraid to call Jane Gallagher, and he ends up insulting Sally Hayes.

Cut off from his peers, Holden sympathizes with young children who are isolated—the little boy walking on the street edge with cars racing by while his parents are oblivious to the danger, the crying child at the movie theater whose needs are ignored by his mother, and Allie, whose dead body lies alone in the cemetery. (Bungert, 181)

Salinger emphasizes Holden's neurotic condition and his alienation from the world by using the motif of madness (Strauch, 155) to contrast the sane, phony people with crazy, pure Holden. (Pinsker, *Innocence Under Pressure,* 33) Holden identifies with madmen, stating that he likes the Gerasene demoniac of the New Testament—the demon-possessed, tomb-dwelling, mentally ill Legion. He confesses, "If you want to know the truth, the guy I like best in the Bible, next to Jesus, was that lunatic and all, that lived in the tombs and kept cutting himself with stones." (99)

Holden often also calls himself a "madman." At Pencey Prep, when he is upset with Stradlater, Holden says he "went right on smoking like a madman." (42) He "apologizes like a madman" many times—when he offends the woman he picks up in the hotel bar, (73) when he accidentally blows smoke in the nuns' faces, (113) and when he is rude to Sally. (134) He concludes his analysis of his disastrous date with Sally by stating, "I'm a madman." (134) "Crazy" is another word Holden frequently uses: he "nearly went crazy" when he found out Stradlater had a date with Jane; (34) after the encounter with Maurice and Sunny, he states, "I'm crazy"; (103) and he tells Sally that he is "crazy" when he begs her to escape from the world with him. Thus, the motif of "madness" is used to show that those who refuse to conform to the world and find the world a scary, lonely place can, like Holden, truly become crazy.

By the end of the novel, misfit, isolated Holden is sent to a psychoanalyst who fails to understand Holden's disillusionment with the world. Thus, Salinger shows that the "isolation, anxiety, the modern sickness of soul turns out to be the given irremediable condition of our lives." (Rowe, 92)

Search for Meaning in Life

The Catcher in the Rye is a story of "the plight of the idealist in the modern world" of falsity and superficiality. (Trowbridge, 22) Without adult role models, Holden is almost doomed to fail. He is surrounded by adult males who cannot help him: a father who is absent; a big brother who has "prostitute[d]" (2) himself; and educators who are boring (Mr. Spencer), hypocritical (Headmaster Haas), or sexually threatening (Mr. Antolini). The adult women in his life (his mother, Mrs. Spencer, Mrs. Morrow, and Mrs. Antolini), although loving and nurturing, are also unable to help him because they have no grasp on reality. Both Stradlater and Carl Luce, his male peers, are superficially macho, while Ackley is merely a pimply slob. Most of the girls—Faith Cavendish, the three dancers from Seattle, Lillian, prostitute Sunny, and Sally Hayes—are irritating phonies.

What Holden wants in the midst of a corrupt and phony world is a real relationship. It is only when he is with Phoebe that he is able to reconnect with the human race in a limited way. However, as critic Helen Weinberg points out, the full realization of a spiritual self is not attainable in a corrupt and phony society. (65)

Analysis

Narration and Voice

One of the reasons *The Catcher in the Rye* has remained a popular book for more than fifty years is that readers empathize with Holden, who tells his story from the first-person point of view. Holden talks directly to the reader, engaging one's sympathy: "If you really want to hear about it." (1) And it continues to the last sentences: "Don't ever tell anybody anything. If you do, you start missing everybody." (214) In between, he constantly chats with the reader. For example, early in the book, remembering he has not mentioned his expulsion from school, he remarks, "I forgot to tell you about that." (4) After the incident with

Maurice and Sunny, he confesses, "I felt so depressed, you can't imagine." (98) As he happily watches Phoebe riding the carousel, he declares that it is so pleasant that "I wish you could've been there." (213) The confessional nature of the story also adds to the sense of familiarity as Holden embraces the reader as his confidant: "I'll just tell you about this madman stuff that happened to me around last Christmas." (1) This intimacy helps readers identify with Holden and embrace him as a good, decent person.

Also helping establish the intimacy with the reader is Holden's slangy, repetitious, non-literary style of speech. His use of the teenage vernacular of the 1950s has been praised from the time of the book's publication. Although many reviewers found the book's language "daring," "obscene," or even "blasphemous," it was hailed as the "authentic" informal speech of an "intelligent, educated, Northeastern American adolescent." (Costello, 93)

David P. Costello notes two main attributes of Holden's realistic language. First, Holden ends many of this thoughts very loosely by adding short phrases that often do not add to the meaning of the sentence. One expression he likes is "and all": "he's my brother and all"; (1) "It was December and all"; (4) Phoebe would "walk right between us, like a lady and all." (68) Phrases he uses to prove his sincerity are, "I really did," "It really was," or "if you want to know the truth," as in, "My nerves were shot. They really were," (51) and, "I felt so d--n happy, if you want to know the truth." (213; Costello, 94–96)

The second major characteristic of Holden's speech is his use of vulgarity. He draws upon the divine name and derivations of it ("for G--'s sake" and "g----m," for example) to express a variety of feelings: pleasure ("my g----m hunting cap," [45]) disapproval ("ya g----m moron," [44]) or indifference ("g----m theater tickets"[116]). He also likes crude language—however, the curse words that are considered most obscene are not part of Holden's speech. They are used only in reference to graffiti that Holden attempts to "rub off" with his hand. (262) Slang words, such as "crap," "crazy," "killed," and "old," are all overused by the teenage protagonist. The informal and colloquial language, filled with crude, slangy, imprecise words, is typical of some adolescent speakers, which makes the reader feel connected to Holden. (Costello, 96–104)

Characterization

Readers' identification with Holden Caulfield has long been noted. In 1959, Granville Hicks wrote that there are "millions of young Americans who feel closer to Salinger than to any other writer." (91) Mark Silverberg believes there are two main reasons for this identification. One is that Holden's feelings of anxiety and uncertainty are typical emotions experienced by adolescents; therefore, "some readers . . . find comfort in the belief that their experience is shared by a community of respondents." (Silverberg, 14) Another group identifies "with Holden in exactly the *opposite* way. These readers feel that their experience and Holden's experience are special because they are *unique*." (Silverberg, 14)

Silverberg points out that there are two particular stories of Holden that readers identify with: "the story of the sensitive outsider and of the boy who refused to grow up." (20) As a sensitive outsider who longs to escape the superficial world by living in a cabin in the remote New England hills, or by going west to live as a "deaf-mute," Holden speaks for disaffected young people who see the world as phony or indifferent. For these people, *The Catcher in the Rye,* as Ian Hamilton writes, became "the book all brooding adolescents had to buy, the indispensable manual from which cool styles of disaffection could be borrowed." (155)

The second type of identification has to do with "Peter Pan readings" about a boy who refuses to grow up. (Silverberg, 24) Holden is a symbol of a spontaneous, idealistic, innately good child. He generously gives money to the nuns who have little; he worries about the ducks when the water freezes; he is concerned about his mother's feelings if he should die; he shows kindness to the pimply, unhygienic Ackley; and he sympathizes with girls. (Gwynn and Blotner, 87) But probably the way he shows the most goodness and concern is seen in his decision to be a "catcher in the rye" to save young, innocent children.

By the end of the novel, Holden realizes that he cannot escape society and remain an outsider, nor can he remain in an innocent childlike state by getting rid of all the bad things in the world. He abandons his desire to go west to play a "deaf-mute" and get a job pumping gas. Ironically, Holden ends up in the West, but it is not the free West of "rugged individuality, self-reliance, and boundless freedom" (Pinsker, *Innocence Under Pressure,* 89) that he envisioned. Instead, he is confined in a mental hospital where he is expected to learn how to reenter society, not escape from it.

Structure

Holden's story is in "the form of a pilgrimage, a journey in which the character enters, intentionally or accidentally, a previously inexperienced world, and then reenters his own world to find both it and himself profoundly altered." (Mills, 46) It begins and ends in a mental hospital on the West Coast. In between this frame, his story is organized into three main sections. The first, chapters 1–7, takes place at Pencey Prep. Holden is immediately seen as alienated, standing alone while the other students attend a football game, telling readers that after he lost the fencing team's equipment, "the whole team ostracized me the whole way back on the train,"(3) and confessing that he has flunked out of school. In this first section, he sees the dishonesty of the world as exemplified by such things as his school's image, his snobby professor, and his womanizing roommate. As a result, he flees from this phony environment.

Chapter 8 serves as a bridge between Pencey and Manhattan. On his train ride, Holden tries to impress Mrs. Morrow by both copying and condemning the adult world.

The second part, chapters 9–20, concerns Holden's return to Manhattan and his manic-depressive attempts to find meaning in life. In his haphazard, frenzied wanderings around New York, he meets old acquaintances and makes new ones, which gives him more exposure to phony people. As he attempts to have sexual encounters (with Faith Cavendish, the three girls from Seattle, the prostitute Sunny, and Sally Hayes), goes to various performances, visits bars, and walks the streets, he becomes more and more depressed. Holden's nights on the town in Manhattan leave him exhausted and hungover.

The third section, chapters 21--25, also takes place in Manhattan as Holden tries to recover the world of innocence through two visits. First he visits Phoebe, his honest, caring, ten-year-old sister, and tells her that he wants to save all children by being a "catcher in the rye." However, he comes to realize that this is not a workable ideal because children cannot remain in a state of innocence; they have to go over the cliff into adulthood. Next he turns to Mr. Antolini, the "best teacher" (174) who had protected the young James Castle in the past. Although this former teacher clearly cares about Holden and almost understands Holden's misery, Holden runs from him when he fears Mr. Antolini is "making a flitty pass" (194) at him. Both of these visits make him realize that innocence cannot be preserved. Totally disillusioned, he wanders around in a figurative death, afraid that he will fall into a void each time he crosses the street. Now, instead of saving the world by protecting the children, Holden wants to reject the world and shut himself off from evil by becoming a "deaf-mute" in the West. It is Phoebe who rescues him from this total withdrawal by refusing to let him go alone. When he sees her grasping for the gold ring on the carousel, a promise of life, he realizes he needs to let go of his fantasies of either saving or rejecting the world. Rather, he recognizes that children need to grow to adulthood. Some may be defeated and fall off the horse as they reach for the gold ring, but some may get the gold ring. In chapter 26, the story ends as it began, in the West, where Holden is trying to learn to connect with people, which he does to some extent, for he says, "I sort of miss everybody I told about." (214)

Symbols

Symbols—material objects such as colors, objects, or characters used to represent abstract ideas—are used throughout the novel.

1. **The "Catcher in the Rye."** Robert Burns' poem "Comin' Thro' the Rye" provides the title for the book. It appears in chapter 16, when Holden is walking the streets of New York and sees a young child innocently singing the song, and again in chapter 22, when Holden tells Phoebe that he wants to be a protector of children as a "catcher in the rye": "I keep picturing all these little kids playing some game in this big field of rye and all. . . . And I'm standing on the edge of some crazy cliff. What I have to do, I have to catch everybody if they start to go over the cliff." (173)

   Phoebe, however, points out that Holden has used the wrong words: Burns' poem reads, "If a body *meet* a body coming through the rye," not "If a body *catch* a body." Ironically, the words are changed to indicate an action that must be stopped, the plummeting over the edge of the cliff. Holden plans to protect innocence and live in an ideal world. But Robert Burns talks about change—meeting a person, daring to seize the moment, and having an intimate encounter with someone.

2. **Preparatory School Life.** Both Pencey Prep and Elkton Hills, Holden's last two schools, are symbols of the phony adult world. Holden rails against the false advertisements for Pencey Prep showing "some hot-shot guy on a horse" (2) when the school has no horses. Likewise, he hates the school motto, "Since 1888 we have been molding boys into splendid, clear-thinking young men," (2) because he sees no one being molded into a "splendid and clear-thinking" (2) person. Instead, most of the boys are like Stradlater, who looks good and seems charming but who is a womanizer, a "secret slob," (27) and a cheat who gets Holden to write his English paper for him. Furthermore, the boys at the school are "mean guys," (167) Holden tells Phoebe, a fact corroborated by James Castle's suicide at Elkton Hills. Holden thus sees these fashionable prep schools as corrupt.

3. **The Subway Map.** Lost in New York with the fencing team, just like he is lost in life, Holden looks for a guide. Even though he sees a map in the subway, he cannot easily understand it. So engrossed is he in trying to follow the map that he leaves the team's foils and equipment behind so they cannot play. This parallels his life: he looks hard to find the way to live in a phony world, but he is unable to succeed.

4. **Holden's Red Hunting Cap.** Bright red with an extralong bill and huge earflaps, this unfashionable cap, which Holden bought in New York on the Saturday morning he lost the school's fencing equipment, is a symbol of his individuality, for he wants to be different from every phony he encounters. Therefore, the

hat, which he wears backwards like a baseball catcher, helps develop the theme of alienation. This cap may also remind him of love and innocence, for it is red, the same color as Allie and Phoebe's hair, the two young, innocent siblings Holden loves.

5. **Allie's Baseball Glove.** The fielder's glove for left-handed Allie shows both Allie's individuality and Holden's love for his dead brother, and is, therefore, used to develop the themes of phoniness and death. Knowing how boring it can be as a baseball fielder, Allie wrote poems in green ink all over his mitt so he would have something to read while standing in the field. The glove, very special to Holden, has been seen by only one person other than Allie's family members: Jane Gallagher. As might be expected, superficial, phony Stradlater thinks an essay written on this memento of an authentic person is a stupid topic.

6. **Manhattan Locations.** The places Holden goes to in Manhattan are representative of life. Central Park with its lagoon that is "partly frozen and partly not frozen" (154) is an image for the hostile, indifferent world as Holden views it, while the ducks and fish are like people who have to survive. Several times, Holden expresses concern for the ducks, and sometimes the fish, wondering what happens to them in winter when the lagoon freezes. Since they both reappear every spring, they show that no matter how harsh their environment, it is possible for them to persevere. This is a lesson Holden needs

to learn: how to survive in a hostile, phony environment. The question about the ducks also reveals Holden's concerns about "things that get lost in the whirlwinds of history, mindless consumption, and general phoniness." (Heman, 65) Although they seem immaterial to the masses of people, such as the cab driver, they are important to sensitive Holden.

Broadway and 42nd Street, the locations of the greatest theatrical performances in America, are symbols of false lovers of the arts and relate to the theme of phoniness to Holden. Holden takes Sally, "the queen of the phonies," (116) to a Broadway theater, a gathering place for phonies. Holden hates intermission, when he spends time with the "jerks," complaining, "You never saw so many phonies in all your life, everybody smoking their ears off and talking about the play so that everybody could hear and know how sharp they were." (126) These locations are also symbolic of phony actors, such as the Lunts and Sir Laurence Olivier, who "never act like people." (117) If any actor is good, "you can always tell he *knows* he's good, and that spoils it." (117) So concerned is Holden about how a performer acts that he cannot enjoy the play: "I keep worrying about whether he's going to do something phony every minute." (117)

Radio City Music Hall represents almost all that Holden hates about phony art that panders to the audience. Here, Holden sees the Rockettes, who "were kicking their heads off"; (137) a Christmas pageant that is neither religious nor beautiful to him; (137) and a "putrid" war film (138) that romanticizes combat.

The Museum of Natural History, with its displays of dead things, stands for the type of world Holden thinks he would like to live in—a place where nothing changes. He "loved that d---n museum" (120) because "everything always stayed right where it was. Nobody'd move." (121) A "nice and peaceful" (204) place, Holden wants life to imitate the museum, for the changes he has endured have been heartbreaking or terrifying, especially the death of Allie.

The carousel at Central Park relates to life and pleasure and innocence. It is a beautiful motorized merry-go-round with painted horses that move up and down. On the outer edge is a gold ring several inches in diameter. As the children ride, the daring ones reach out to try to grab it as they go by. It is a risky move because they could fall off their horses. However, those who grasp it are usually rewarded with a prize, such as a free ride or a stuffed animal. The gold ring that Phoebe is reaching for is a symbol of hope, a desirable end result, but it is also a symbol of risk. Holden's recognition that he needs to let Phoebe try to grab the gold ring is a major insight for him. He realizes that he cannot be Phoebe's constant protector, her "catcher in the rye," but that she needs to make her own decisions and take her own risks.

Literary Criticism of the Novel

Published in mid-July 1951, *The Catcher in the Rye* was so much in demand that it was reprinted five times in July, three times in August, and twice in September. (Gutwillig, 4) Two weeks after it was published, it was number fourteen on the *New York Times* bestseller list, and by October, it had risen to the number four spot, the highest position the book reached. (Gutwillig, 4) It stayed on the bestseller list for thirty weeks. (Alexander, 154)

In the first months after its publication, there were at least two hundred reviews of *The Catcher in the Rye.* (Laser and Fruman, "Early Reviews," 17) Although some were favorable, it was not acclaimed as a great achievement or a book of lasting quality. Clifton Fadiman of the Book-of-the-Month Club, which had selected Salinger's novel as its main selection for July, wrote an exceedingly positive review: "That rare miracle of fiction has again come to pass: a human being has been created out of ink, paper and the imagination." (quoted in Laser and Fruman, "Early Reviews," 7) Paul Engle, in the *Chicago Sunday Tribune Magazine of Books* found the story"engaging and believable . . . full of right observation and sharp insight," (5) while Harrison Smith, in the *Saturday Review of Literature* raved that the novel is "remarkable and absorbing . . . a book to be read thoughtfully and more than once." (28)

However, most reviewers qualified their praise with criticism. Some faulted the plot, finding it "too long," "monotonous," "predictable and boring," (Jones, 176) and "too formless," (R. D. Charques, quoted in Laser and Fruman, "Early Reviews," 17) with "no point of view, and no target to aim at but [Salinger] himself." (Poster, 27) Other critics disliked the protagonist, asserting that "the book as a whole is disappointing . . . [because] there is too much of [Holden]," (Goodman, 23) who is a "decisive failure." (Breit, 82)

It was the language, however, that received the most criticism. Virgilia Peterson, in the *New York Herald Tribune Book Review,* censured the vulgar words, which, coming "from the mouths of the very young and protected . . . sound peculiarly offensive." (4) Reinforcing this point was

T. Morris Longstreth of the *Christian Science Monitor,* who called it a book of "immorality and perversion" (31) "not fit for children to read." (30) *Catholic World* also objected to the language, asserting that Holden's character "is made monotonous and phony by the formidably excessive use of amateur swearing and coarse language." (154) Across the ocean, the *London Times Literary Supplement* condemned "the endless stream of blasphemy and obscenity" which "palls after the first chapter." (quoted in Laser and Fruman, "Early Reviews," 17)

Even though *The Catcher in the Rye* sold well from the beginning, critics did not agree on the merits of the book. A number thought the public esteemed it too highly, including George Steiner who denounced what he called "The Salinger Industry," (82–85) and Alfred Kazin, who mockingly called Salinger "everybody's favorite," (67–75) stating that Salinger's popularity was not due to his greatness but to his ability to appeal to bored American sophisticates. (75) However, others were more favorable, viewing the novel as a minor classic. Still others placed it in the mainstream of American literature, referring to it as an "epic" (Heiserman and Miller, 32) or a "quest," (Kaplan, 43) and describing Holden as a "saint." (Hassan, 260–289; Baumbach, 55–64)

In spite of the mixed responses, in the last half century the novel "has enjoyed a readership that has transcended the boundaries of age, education, and culture, a phenomenon unparalleled in the history of modern and contemporary literature." (Salzberg, "Introduction," 1) In America, *The Catcher in the Rye* sold over three million copies in the first thirteen years. (Whitfield, 77) By the end of the 1960s, Facts on File listed *The Catcher in the Rye* as "one of the leading 25 bestsellers since 1895." (Sublette, 132) As the century moved forward, the novel continued to sell well. It has had over seventy printings and has been translated into thirty languages. (Whitfield, 77)

Regardless of its popularity, *The Catcher in the Rye* has been a target for censors since the mid–1950s for four main reasons: people object to the "crude, profane, obscene" language; they find the "scandalous" episodes inappropriate for teenagers; they feel that Holden, "a phony himself," is not an appropriate role model; (Corbett, 135, 137, 138) and they disapprove of Holden's attacks on American values. From 1966 to 1975, forty-one attempts were made to keep *The Catcher in the Rye* out of public educational institutions, (Green, 332) making it "the most frequently banned book in schools" during these years. (Karolides, Bald, and Sova, 366)

In a variety of states in America, there have been numerous calls to ban *The Catcher in the Rye* from public libraries and schools. In 1960, it was removed from the library and the recommended reading list in a San Jose, California, high school. (Salzman, "Introduction," 14) That same year, teachers in Louisville, Kentucky, and Tulsa, Oklahoma, were threatened with dismissal after they assigned the novel to their high school classes. (Salzman, "Introduction," 14; Haight and Grannis, 92) In 1962, when the novel was assigned as supplemental reading for an eleventh-grade class in Temple City, California, a parent objected to the "crude, profane, and obscene" language and condemned the novel for its attack on patriotism, "home life, [the] teaching profession, religion, and so forth." (Laser and Fruman, "Not Suitable for Temple City," 124–129) In 1963, parents of high school students in Columbus, Ohio, requested that the school board ban *The Catcher in the Rye* because it was "anti-white" and "obscene." (Karolides, Bald, and Sova, 366)

In the 1970s, citizens across the country became even more vocal about removing Salinger's novel from high school reading lists, charging that the book was "explicitly pornographic" and "immoral," and contained "filthy and profane" language that promoted "premarital sex, homosexuality and perversion." (Karolides, Bald, and Sova, 367) In 1972, Massachusetts parents claimed that no young person could read this "totally filthy, totally depraved and totally profane" book "without being scarred." (Salzman, "Introduction," 15). It was banned in the high schools of Issaquah, Washington, in 1978 when a citizen found 785 profanities and charged that including the novel in the syllabus was "part of an overall communist plot." (Whitfield, 82) Schools in Pennsylvania, Michigan, and New Jersey also demanded that the novel be banished. (Karolides, Bald, and Sova, 366–367)

The book continued to be challenged in the 1980s and 1990s. Calls for its banishment came from communities across the country—from California in the West to New Hampshire in the East, from Florida in the South to Wisconsin and North Dakota in the North. (Karolides, Bald, and Sova, 367)

Although parents have objected to the book generation after generation, teachers have found it so compelling that they continue to place it on required reading lists for high schoolers. Students have eagerly embraced the book. It is a work which has had wide appeal to different generations and different social groups. It spoke to the "antiestablishmentarian attitude of fifties intellectuals," (Seelye, 25) and it became the mouthpiece for the counterculture of the activist anti-Vietnam War generation of the 1960s. In the following decades this counterculture became the culture of the universities and the media.

For over half a century, *The Catcher in the Rye* has appealed to people of various ages and cultures. To this day, the novel has not lost its appeal for two main reasons. First, readers identify with Holden, and second, it is well written. Holden, who would now be an old man if he were real, continues to live as a troubled, witty teenager in the hearts of readers throughout the country and around the world.

THE TOWER — *Jeanne Singer*
The novella of the month; a youthful idyll

STRAWBERRIES IN JANUARY — *Vivian Connell*
A new young Irish writer in an unusual vein

THERE MUST BE SOMEONE — *Lionel Wiggam*
An American poet's story of a lonely young woman

THE YOUNG FOLKS — *J. D. Salinger*

POET'S GRIEF — *Emmett Gowen*

THE YEARS GO BY — *Alphabelle Daily*
A tender morsel from Missouri STORY readers will appreciate

TRACKS IN THE SNOW — *Edward Havill*

EASTER EGG — *Frank Brookhouser*
An unforgettable story of a boy's first girl

HONEYMOON — *V. G. Calderon*
Another little tale by a kin of the great Calderon

SURVEY OF REVIEWS — *The new books: Plus & Minus*

40 CENTS

STORY MAGAZINE WAS, FITTINGLY, THE FIRST MAGAZINE TO PUBLISH A STORY BY J. D. SALINGER.

Chapter 4

Salinger's Stories

The Early Stories

"THE YOUNG FOLKS," J. D. SALINGER'S first published story, appeared in Whit Burnett's *Story* in 1940, when Salinger was only twenty-one. After the launching of his career, Salinger continued to produce stories, not even slowing down during World War II, for he carried a typewriter with him on his campaigns. Salinger found much financial success as he moved from small periodicals to widely circulated national magazines, such as *Collier's* and the *Saturday Evening Post.* Beginning in 1948, he began selling almost all of his stories to the prestigious *New Yorker.* Altogether, Salinger published thirty stories from 1940 to 1953. Nine of these he selected for *Nine Stories,* a collection printed in 1953. Of the twenty-one stories left only in magazines, Salinger, in an interview with the *New York Times* in 1974, said that he "wanted them to die a perfectly natural death." (quoted in Alexander, 250)

The stories he chose to preserve were all stories published after the war, between 1948 and 1953; all but "Down at the Dinghy" and "De Daumier-Smith's Blue Period" had appeared in the *New Yorker.* Reverberating with the costs of war in human lives, they deal with "genius, spiritual integrity, moral corruption, and the occasional ability of innocence to transform our lives." (Dominic Smith, 639–640) Although arranged in the order of their publication, the stories are loosely interconnected. Not only are many of the characters looking for relief from their alienation, which is often caused by a lack of love, but many receive enlightenment in response to a seemingly insignificant event or object.

For Salinger, enlightenment is based mostly on his beliefs in Zen Buddhism and Vedanta, a study that he began after World War II. Salinger begins *Nine Stories* with a famous Zen koan: "We know the sound of two hands clapping. / But what is the sound of one hand clapping?" The word Zen means thinking, contemplating, meditating; the koan is a question which causes a person to think. Like all koans, this one has no right answer. Instead, Salinger is inviting readers to think of his nine stories "as riddles without any obvious solutions . . . they are points of departure for thinking, questioning, meditating." (Mills, 50)

In *Nine Stories*, Salinger explores how some people estranged from the world can find reconciliation or even redemption, which gives them the ability to survive in a hostile world, while others try to escape from the perverse world, an attempt that either leads them to disaster or true enlightenment.

"A Perfect Day for Bananafish" (*New Yorker*, January 31, 1948)

This opening story, one of the best known in America in the years following World War II, consists of two major scenes. The first takes place in a hotel room in Florida where Muriel Glass talks by phone to her mother in New York about her husband Seymour's strange behavior. The second scene occurs on the beach where Seymour takes Sybil Carpenter, who seems to be five or six years old, into the ocean on her float and talks to her about the sad story of bananafish who die of banana fever after swimming into a hole, gorging on bananas, and becoming too fat to swim out. The story ends as Seymour returns to his hotel room where Muriel lies sleeping and shoots himself through the right temple.

Critical responses to the story revolve around two primary questions: What does a bananafish symbolize? And why does Seymour kill himself?

Although critics generally agree that the bananafish story has to do with the struggle between materialism and spirituality, they are not united on who the bananafish is. Some, including James Lundquist and Eberhard Alsen, think that common, materialistic people, like Muriel, are bananafish. However, others see Seymour as a bananafish. William Wiegand calls Seymour "a bananafish himself, [who] has become so glutted with sensation that he cannot swim out into society again," (125) while James E. Miller Jr. believes that Seymour's "senses have been ravaged by the physical world, and he has found himself entrapped and must die." (28–29)

As a result of these different interpretations, readers view Seymour's suicide in widely different ways, suggesting that it was caused by his war experience, or by being mismatched with Muriel, or by his inability, as a spiritual man, to tolerate a materialistic world. (Mills, 57) Thus some, like Alsen, feel his suicide is a necessary act in order "to escape from the world of the bananafish." (*Glass Stories,* 16) However, Warren French finds it "a demented act" (*J. D. Salinger,* 83) of a petulant husband who wants "to make the well-composed Muriel pay attention to him." (*Revisited*, 66) Still others regard his suicide as a positive action. Miller writes that "his suicide is a release for [Muriel] to engage life again at a level she can apprehend, and a release for himself from a physicality that has simply ceased to be endurable." (29) Lundquist, after explaining that suicide "does not have the negative connotations in Buddhism that it does in Christianity," concludes that Seymour's suicide is "an act of protest, a protest against the phoniness embodied by Muriel and Miami Beach." (87)

"Uncle Wiggily in Connecticut" (*New Yorker*, March 20, 1948)

Phoniness is the subject of this story about an unhappy suburban housewife, Eloise, who, as she is drinking with her old college roommate, Mary Jane, reveals the reason for her antagonism toward her daughter and her husband. She remembers her life in the "nice" world when she enjoyed a brief romance with a soldier named Walt, who had imaginatively called her injured ankle "Uncle Wiggily." When he was killed in a freak accident after the war, Eloise married Lew. Now, trapped in the "phony" world of Connecticut, "she is reduced to a kind of death-in-life that has withered her into a cold, high-handed, alienated being." (French, *Revisited,* 69) In a moment of enlightenment, she realizes that the "nice" girl she used to be has been given new life in her imaginative daughter, Ramona, and she tucks the blankets around her sleeping child. Critics disagree on the meaning of the story's conclusion. Some see Eloise condemned to her bleak world of self-pity, while others think she is being restored to her "nice self."

This is the only Salinger story which was made into a motion picture. Called *My Foolish Heart,* the Samuel Goldwyn film, released in 1950, starred Susan Hayward and Dana Andrews. Salinger was so upset with the changes made to his story that he has refused to sell screen or television rights to any of his other works.

"Just Before the War with the Eskimos" (*New Yorker*, June 5, 1948)

Although again dealing with the "nice" versus the "phony" worlds, the third story is more optimistic. Ginnie Mannox, a "nice" girl, is angry with her tennis partner, Selena, and has come to her apartment to wait for her half of the fare for the cab ride they shared. Here she meets Selena's brother, Franklin, a sensitive young man who has been kept out of the war due to a bad heart, and has instead worked in an airplane factory. He has been rejected by girls and appears to be about to enter into a homosexual relationship. He sees war as absurd, as meaningless as fighting against the Eskimos. Trapped in a loveless world, he reaches out to Ginnie by offering her a leftover chicken sandwich; she accepts and keeps it, refusing to throw it away.

Again, the ending is unclear. It may show futility as Ginnie "nurtures" a sandwich that is the beginning of a doomed relationship, or there may be some sort of hope that human connection can bring about a reconciliation with the world.

"The Laughing Man" (*New Yorker*, March 19, 1949)

This story looks at the sadness of a breakup. The narrator tells a story about his childhood when he was a nine-year-old member of the Comanche Club, led by John Gedsudski, a young law student. He entertains the boys by reciting the adventures of "The Laughing Man," a type of deformed Robin Hood, his face having been misshapen when he was a child. When John Gedsudski falls in love with Mary Hudson, the stories of the "The Laughing Man" are energetic. But when John and Mary quarrel and separate, through no explained cause, John sends his hero into captivity and death, shocking the young narrator. Although John Gedsudski does not kill himself in defeat, he uses his bitter experience to teach his young charges "a startling object lesson in not expecting too much from life." (French, *Revisited,* 74)

"Down at the Dinghy" (*Harper's* Magazine, April 1949)

At the center of the collection comes a story dealing with the social issue of ethnic prejudice. A four-year-old boy, Lionel Tannenbaum, has run away to the family dinghy, and his mother, Boo Boo Glass Tannenbaum, finally persuades him to leave the boat. She discovers that he ran away after overhearing the housekeeper call his father a "kike," which he mistakes for "one of those things which go up in the air." (86)

This piece is generally regarded as the poorest story in the collection. Lundquist calls it "the low point in the book"; (98) French considers it "the most contrived and unconvincing in the collection"; (*Revisited,* 74) and Maxwell Geismer criticizes it as "a tricky little bit of anti-anti Semitism." (200)

"For Esmé—with Love and Squalor" (*New Yorker,* April 8, 1950)

Many critics agree with Frederick L. Gwynn and Joseph L. Blotner that this story is "the high point of [Salinger's] art." (4) It is the tale of the love the narrator feels for an ideal human being and the squalor she requests in a story written solely for her.

Like "Bananafish," this story has two primary scenes. It begins with an introduction in which the narrator writes that he has received an invitation to a wedding in England. Even though he cannot attend, he says he has "jotted down a few revealing notes on the bride as [he] knew her almost six years ago." (87)

The first scene takes place in a British town during World War II where the narrator is stationed with the American army. One day he meets and has tea with Esmé, a thirteen-year-old English girl who wears an enormous wristwatch, and her five-year-old brother, Charles. With them he discovers human warmth.

The second scene occurs in Bavaria after the war. The events in this scene are so painful that the narrator tells the story in the third person, as Sergeant X, who is recovering from a nervous breakdown. Written on the flyleaf of a book, he finds the words, "Dear God, life is hell," (105) and adds, "Fathers and teachers, I ponder 'What is hell?' I maintain that it is the suffering of being unable to love." (105) Experiencing that loss, he feels like he is in hell. Looking through his mail, he finds a package from Esmé that contains a letter and her dearest possession—her father's watch. Esmé's unexpected gifts renew Sergeant X's dark spirit, and he is able to feel love, find refreshment in sleep, and start restoring his faculties.

This "wonderfully moving story" (Steiner, 83) is one of the few by Salinger in which the "nice" world triumphs over the "phony" or squalid one. Both Esmé and Sergeant X show that "there is a way to be immersed in squalor, recognize it as such, and eventually overcome it." (Wenke, "Sergeant X," 254) Sergeant X's world is so full of human misery that he is unable to love, but the fact that he is writing the story "provides the completion of the psychological therapy which began when he read Esmé's letter and fell asleep." (Wenke, "Sergeant X," 254) Esmé represents the highest state of a person who chooses to live in a squalid society, for she shows loyalty to her family, compassion to a lonely American soldier, and love for future generations which she will have after her marriage. Esmé is one of the remarkable people who is able to live a meaningful, loving life in a corrupt world.

"Pretty Mouth and Green My Eyes" (*New Yorker*, July 14, 1951)

This tale of human squalor through marital betrayal and self-deception is one of Salinger's most "bitter, cynical stories" that plunges readers "into the pit of modern urban hell." (French, *Revisited*, 79) It consists of two telephone conversations that a young lawyer, Arthur, makes to an older lawyer in the same firm, Lee, following a cocktail party. In the first call, Arthur asks if Lee saw his wife leave the party; in the second call, he tries to save face by telling Lee that his wife has come home. Ironically, the older lawyer is in bed with the younger man's wife during both calls.

The ending is unresolved—there may be more acts of betrayal or the affair may end. Most critics do not see this as a very successful story because "a story so heavily loaded with irony could not possibly succeed." (Lundquist, 102)

"De Daumier-Smith's Blue Period" (*London World Review*, May 1952)

The longest of the nine stories, this one is told by a first-person narrator who recalls a traumatic time in his life thirteen years earlier that ended with redemption through a mystical Zen experience.

Mourning the death of his mother and living with his stepfather in New York, the narrator, sickened by life, is so isolated that Salinger does not even state his real name. Wanting to escape the world, he falsifies his name, his past, and his qualifications, and gets a job at an art academy correspondence school in Montreal. He finds most of his students to be bad artists. However, one is a talented nun to whom he writes a long, intimate letter, causing her to withdraw from school. He expels the other students.

Depressed, De Daumier-Smith takes a walk and has a mystic experience as he is blinded by a vision of "a shimmering field of exquisite, twice-blessed, enamel flowers" (250) in the window of an orthopedic appliances shop, causing him to see life in a new way. Embracing a oneness with the world, he reinstates his bad students and sees all the world as sacred, as would a nun. A few days later, the school is closed for being improperly licensed, and De Daumier-Smith returns to his former life with his stepfather. As Miller explains, he "is symbolically rejoining the human race; he has made the decision to be more than just a 'visitor' in the physical universe." (25)

"Teddy" (*New Yorker*, January 31, 1953)

Salinger's last story in the collection is another tale of mysticism. Ten-year-old Theodore McArdle, on an ocean trip with his disagreeable parents and his six-year-old sister, Booper, is a gifted boy who, because of his many reincarnations, has the ability to see the future, including when a person will die. In his conversation with passenger Bob Nicholson, Teddy reveals that he considers death a minor matter because "All you do is get the heck out of your body when you die," (193) and then you become reincarnated into a new one. Although he foresees that his sister may kill him by pushing him into an empty swimming pool, he passively goes down to the pool. The narrator records that there was an "all-piercing, sustained scream—clearly coming from a small, female child," (198) but the ending is not clear—whether Teddy jumped to his death, was pushed by Booper, or pushed Booper.

This story falls short in several areas. As Lundquist explains, the characters are undeveloped, the conversation between Teddy and Nicholson "reads like an awkward device to convey Salinger's religious philosophy." (108)

The themes and attitudes conveyed in this story are also unacceptable to many readers. Although Salinger, as a Zen Buddhist, seems to find Teddy's death (if, indeed, he is the one to die) a positive ending since he gains union with the infinite, many people do not share his world view. The idea that the enlightened must escape from the sordid world by overcoming all emotions and passively accepting death does not seem to be a good alternative to living life, even in a sordid world.

Literary Reception of *Nine Stories*

When *Nine Stories* appeared in April 1953, "it seemed to awe, puzzle, and unnerve reviewers in equal measure." (Dominic Smith, 643) Author Eudora Welty had nothing but praise for the collection, calling it "original, first rate, serious, and beautiful." (quoted in Alexander, 173) Others were less enthusiastic. The *Nation's* Alan Barth called the stories "accomplished and effective," and Salinger "a fiction writer of great brilliance" but one who may become an author "of definite and ultimately disappointing limitations." (quoted in Alexander, 172) *Harper's* Gilbert Highet felt the book was "splendid" but warned that Salinger seemed to be writing about the same character in every story. (quoted in Alexander, 172) Those who did not like the collection included Britain's *Times Literary Supplement,* which criticized Salinger as "a writer trapped by his own cleverness," (quoted in Ian Hamilton, 135) and Charles Poore of the *New York Times*, who called the stories "disjointed, uneasy little dreams." (quoted in Dominic Smith, 644)

Because of the reputation of *The Catcher in the Rye* and the media attention, *Nine Stories* was a commercial success. It was soon in ninth position on the *New York Times* bestseller list and remained in the top twenty for three months. Several stories, in particular "Bananafish" and "For Esmé," have been printed in magazines and anthologies throughout the world. (Ian Hamilton, 136)

Some critics believe that "Salinger is undoubtedly a better short-story writer than he is a novelist," (Lundquist, 69) and that *Nine Stories* is "the high point of his foreshortened publishing career." (Dominic Smith, 639) Although *Nine Stories* has never reached the popularity of *The Catcher in the Rye,* it has sold well, remaining in paperback for a half century. Assessing *Nine Stories* fifty years after its publication, Dominic Smith concludes that "personal turmoil, spiritual hunger, and the sheer prowess of Salinger's literary craft, all combined to make this collection the best sort of Zen koan—one that's pleasing and unforgettable in its own right." (649)

The Late Glass Family Stories

Salinger's last stories are "essentially religious in nature." (Alsen, *Glass Stories,* 3) They show how members of the fictional Glass family find insight and strength to live in a chaotic, hostile world. Three of the seven Glass siblings were introduced in *Nine Stories*: Seymour, in "A Perfect Day for Bananafish"; Walt, in "Uncle Wiggily's Connecticut"; and Boo Boo in "Down at the Dinghy." These children of a Jewish-Irish couple, Les and Bessie

Gallagher Glass, are troubled but brilliant young people, appearing on the radio program, "It's a Wise Child." In Salinger's later Glass family stories, four of the children appear as protagonists: Seymour, the family genius and God-seeker who "sees more," and Buddy, the two oldest sons, and Franny and Zooey, the youngest children. With the exception of "Franny," Salinger abandons much of the traditional short-story pattern of characterization, plot, conflict, and resolution, hardly developing secondary characters; discarding rapid dialogue for long conversations, monologues, and readings of letters, diaries, and journals; developing his stories by words instead of actions; and including little or no humor. The themes of his last five stories are similar: the basic rottenness of life, the saving power of love, and the abandonment of the egotistical self. (Mizener, 210)

Franny and Zooey

Franny and Zooey, was originally published as two separate works in the *New Yorker* (January 29, 1955, and May 5, 1957), which were printed together in 1961. Even though the stories do not together read as a novel, both deal with Franny's attempts to find enlightenment and live a spiritual life in the midst of a phony world.

Plot

In "Franny," the heroine visits her college boyfriend Lane Coutell, a pretentious Ivy Leaguer, one weekend over lunch at a local restaurant. She tells him that she is sick of self-centered phonies and pseudointellectuals. Afraid she is "losing her mind" because she is "just sick of ego, ego, ego," (29) she has embraced a book, *The Way of a Pilgrim*, which recommends living a life of praying without ceasing by continually repeating the "Jesus Prayer"—"Lord Jesus Christ, have mercy on me." (36) She wants "to purify [her] whole outlook" (37) so that she will "get to see God." (39)

When Lane expresses skepticism, Franny faints. When she comes to, she finds herself on the couch in the manager's office with Lane sitting next to her. He goes to get her a glass of water and arrange for a cab. Left alone, Franny, her eyes fixed on the ceiling, moves her lips soundlessly in the Jesus Prayer.

"Zooey" takes place on the Monday following Franny's breakdown when she has returned to her family's apartment in New York City. In an attempt to find insight that might enable him to help Franny, Zooey is in the bathtub rereading a four-year-old letter from his older brother, Buddy. Bessie enters the bathroom and pleads with her younger son to talk to Franny. In the next scene, Zooey goes to the living room, where Franny is lying on the couch. Bluntly, he accuses her of selfish withdrawal from life and of misunderstanding the nature of Jesus. But his harshness to her, such as telling her that she is starting "to give off a little stink of piousness" and is leading a "little snotty crusade . . . against everybody," (160–161) only makes her feel worse, so Zooey leaves. Making another attempt to help her, he goes to Seymour and Buddy's room to get inspiration from Seymour's spirit, and reads quotes from Christian, Hindu, Taoist, and Buddhist sources. Inspired, he calls Franny from Seymour's phone, pretending to be Buddy, makes her realize that she is suffering from her inability to love others, and shows her how to rejoin the human race by returning to the theater and acting. Zooey convinces her that she can find Jesus in all people, for the Jesus she was attempting to discover in the Jesus Prayer is just "Seymour's Fat Lady," (201) a member of the audience, who is "Christ Himself." (202) Filled with joy, Franny smiles and falls into a "deep, dreamless sleep." (202)

Analysis

Read alone, "Franny" ends on a sympathetic note as she embraces the Jesus Prayer "in order to withdraw from the crass, materialistic world of people like her boyfriend." (Alsen, 210) However, when "Franny" is combined with "Zooey," her use of this prayer is seen as detrimental because it causes her to withdraw from the world. "Zooey," then, is the story of Franny's recovery from hypercriticism of others, but it is even more the story of Zooey, who becomes exhausted, soaked with sweat, as he saves his sister from her self-induced isolation and realizes himself that spiritual advancement comes through "selfless performance of everyday duties." (Alsen, 228)

The primary theme of this book is love for humanity, which Salinger explores in terms of mysticism and religion. Through the parable of the "Fat Lady," Seymour's term for the uneducated, unappealing, shallow fan of their radio program, "It's a Wise Child," Zooey teaches Franny the Eastern religious belief that everyone is a part of God and therefore merits love and respect. Instead of relying on the "Jesus Prayer," which removes her from other people, Franny learns to embrace others, even those she does not like. Love is also seen in families—the older brothers show concern for Franny and Zooey, Zooey tries to help his sister recover, and Zooey implores Franny to respond to her mother's gesture of love and "drink when somebody brings you a cup of consecrated chicken soup." (196)

The need to embrace gifts and talents, using them to the fullest for self-enhancement, is another theme in this work. In his letter, Buddy admonishes his little brother to "act, Zachary Martin Glass, when and where you want to, . . . but do it with all your might." (68) Zooey passes on this lesson to Franny, telling her to stop getting bogged down by criticizing others and do "the only religious thing" she can do: become "God's actress." (198)

Also examined in this work is the American conformist society of the late 1940s and 1950s. Lane Coutell, who feels satisfied to be "in the right place with an unimpeachably right-looking girl," (11) is condemned as an egotistical phony. Conformist television entertainment in which all stories have sentimental happy endings that appeal to the masses is denounced. And psychotherapists, who became popular after World War II, are described as "ignorant" people who try to make everyone "gloriously normal" (108) and alike.

Critical Reception

The public liked *Franny and Zooey* and, after a cover story appeared in *Time,* it became an immediate bestseller, with 125,000 copies sold in the first two weeks. It stayed on the *New York Times* bestseller list for six months, reaching the number one spot. (Alexander, 212, 214)

Even though the public gladly read it, critics have never been as enthusiastic, largely because of "Zooey." "Franny" continues to be praised as "a textbook example of a well written short story," (Alsen, *Glass Stories,* 22) "a beautifully balanced short story," (Marple, 242) and "the best chapter in the Glass history." (Gwynn and Blotner, 46) But "Zooey" has been faulted from the beginning, disparaged in 1958 as "the longest (29,000 words) and dullest 'short story' ever to appear in the *New Yorker.*" (Gwynn and Blotner, 48) With its loose plot, it is "no novel," (Fiedler, 236), and Salinger's "unwieldy" use of diaries and letters shows his "clouded" artistic judgment. (Marple, 242) Furthermore, it "is just too long; there are too many cigarettes; too many g------s, too much verbal ado about not quite enough." (Updike, 55)

The characters in "Zooey" are condemned as too "cute" to be bearable, (Kazin, 72) whom Salinger loves "more than God loves them . . . to the detriment of artistic moderation." (Updike, 55) Even worse, in this "quasi-religious" (Mary McCarthy, 250) book, the Glass kids are nothing "but Salinger himself, splitting and multiplying like the original amoeba . . . [and] to be confronted with the seven faces of Salinger, all wise and lovable and simple, is to gaze into a terrifying narcissus pool. Salinger's world contains nothing but Salinger, his teachers, and his tolerantly cherished audience." (Mary McCarthy, 248–249)

Salinger's didacticism and beliefs are also attacked. *National Review*'s Joan Didion declared the book "spurious" because of Salinger's "predilection for giving instructions for living." (234) Writer Aleksander Heman condemned Salinger's "belief that any kind of selfishness, self-indulgence, triteness, exploitation, and general ignorance is justifiable, perhaps even desirable, as long as it is a part of some kind of search for enlightenment." (75–76)

Of course, some critics were enthusiastic. *Time* proclaimed it "a glowing minor work" (Skow, 18) and *Saturday Review*'s Granville Hicks commended Salinger for being "at the top of his form." (quoted in Lundquist, 136) The *Christian Century* praised the theme of universal love, applauding Salinger's "almost Pauline understanding of the necessity, nature, and redemptive quality of love." (quoted in Lundquist, 135) Even today, a few young writers appreciate Salinger's book, identifying with Franny (Sohn, 98) or finding it "rich and funny and wise." (Samuels, 133)

But on the whole, the book is seen as "not distinguished art, but a self-improvement tract," (French, *J. D. Salinger*, 148) structurally "something of an embarrassment to readers who had defended and admired the earlier books," (Lundquist, 124) and overall, "almost unbearably tedious" (French, *Revisited*, 95) as it "goes on and on—and on." (Rosenfeld, 86)

Raise High the Roof Beam, Carpenters and Seymour: An Introduction

Raise High the Roof Beam, Carpenters and Seymour: An Introduction, originally printed as two separate stories in the *New Yorker* (November 19, 1955, and June 6, 1959), were published as a book in 1963. Both stories rely on quotations from religious writings, letters, memoirs, and diaries for much of their narrative structure.

Plot

"Raise High the Roof Beam, Carpenters" begins with a Taoist tale about a man named Kao who is able to see inner qualities even though he loses sight of external ones. The story takes place in New York in late May 1942, on the day Seymour is supposed to marry Muriel. Buddy describes how he got a furlough, comes to the wedding, and, when Seymour fails to appear, ends up in a taxicab with the bride's relatives. The Matron of Honor, infuriated with Seymour, states that Muriel's mother must now be totally convinced that Seymour is a "latent homosexual" with a "schizoid personality." (37) The group ends up at Buddy and Seymour's apartment, where Buddy reads Seymour's diary, finding out that his spiritual brother loves the rather vulgar Muriel because of her "undiscriminating heart" (66–67) and her "simplicity." (73) Upset, Buddy drinks some Scotch and serves his guests some Tom Collinses. When the Matron of Honor telephones Muriel's family, she finds out that the bride and groom have eloped. After all of the guests except the deaf-mute leave, Buddy reads more of his brother's diary and passes out. When Buddy wakes up, he is alone in his apartment.

"Seymour: An Introduction" is a haphazard biography of Seymour. Narrator Buddy begins by addressing the "general reader" (96) and stating his philosophy of writing. He next discusses Seymour's essential inner qualities as a poet-seer and a critic by paraphrasing two of his brother's poems, and by quoting Seymour's advice to him to write by using insight and feeling. Next, Buddy describes Seymour as a physical person by looking at sections of his body: hair, ears, eyes, nose, voice, skin, clothes. Buddy concludes his description by telling short stories that explain Seymour's endearing qualities.

Analysis

Eberhard Alsen, in *Salinger's Glass Stories as a Composite Novelist,* offers the most complete analysis of these two stories. He explains that even though "Raise High the Roof Beam, Carpenters" is the story of Seymour's wedding day, Buddy is the protagonist (34) because the story revolves around his two inner conflicts—why his brother did not attend his own wedding and why he chose Muriel as his bride.

The majority of the plot is developed as an external conflict between Buddy and the Matron of Honor. Even though Buddy defends his brother against her attacks, he also realizes she is right that "You can't just barge through life hurting people's feelings whenever you feel like it." (21) Thus, he, like the bride's family, is relieved that Seymour is not truly cruel, for he did not desert his bride but eloped with her.

However, Buddy is still conflicted over Seymour's choice of Muriel, a superficial, materialistic young woman whose hopes and dreams are far different from Seymour's intellectual and spiritual values. His uneasiness at Seymour's marriage to Muriel increases when Muriel's aunt says that Muriel looks like Charlotte Mayhew, the girl Seymour scarred by throwing a stone at her. Rereading his brother's diary, he understands that Seymour feels that his marriage will give him a rebirth. Like Kao of the Taoist tale, Seymour, Buddy realizes, can "see more" than other people, for he understands that Muriel's simplistic inner qualities are things he needs to reunite with people.

The companion piece, "Seymour: An Introduction," appears to be almost formless, a "composition," not a "story" or a "narrative." (French, *Revisited*, 107) Most critics would agree with Clifford Mills that "'Seymour' is a virtual incubator of plot fragments, character ideas, random thoughts, poetic images, and extended metaphors. It is a chaotic warehouse of artistic activity." (64)

However, Alsen finds two story lines, a character sketch of Seymour and the story of Buddy's reasons for writing. (*Glass Stories*, 65) As Buddy is describing Seymour as a poet, a genius, and a God-seeker whose life revolves around spiritual advancement, he also talks about his progress in writing the work: composing the first section in

J. D. Salinger became so famous for his stories and his one novel that he was featured on the cover of *Time* magazine in 1961.

one weekend, becoming sick with hepatitis for nine weeks, writing the section on Seymour as a critic one night, taking seven nights to complete the physical description section, and finishing at 7:30 on a Friday morning just before he has to teach a class. At the end of the story, Buddy comes to a "sudden realization" (204) about his "credo" or belief, understanding that his purpose in life is to relay Seymour's philosophy to his students and readers by writing with spontaneity and intuition.

In spite of Alsen's explanation of the organizational pattern, readers generally remain unimpressed with the work. With its "long, rambling monologue," (Lundquist, 142) and "depressing introductory quotations from Kafka and Kierkegaard about writers' inability to do justice to their subjects," (French, *Revisited*, 107) the "seemingly interminable" section of physical descriptions of Seymour, (French, *J. D. Salinger*, 156) and the didactic ending speech, the story is dismissed.

Critical Reception

When the book was released on January 28, 1963, Salinger received some of the worst reviews of his career. *Newsweek* blasted Salinger and his publisher for printing these two stories in one volume, complaining that they "are nearly as great a gyp artistically as they are financially." (quoted in Alexander, 226) Irving Howe of the *New York Times Book Review* attacked the book as "hopelessly prolix" and "marred" by the writer's "self-indulgence." (quoted in Alexander, 226) *New Republic*'s John Wain faulted Buddy as "a bore. He is prolix, obsessed with his subject, given to rambling confidences, and altogether the last person to be at the helm in an enterprise like this." (quoted in Lundquist, 146–147)

These reviews of the book match other assessments of the stories. When it was first published in 1958, "Raise High the Roof Beams, Carpenters" was condemned as "long, didactic and largely unsymmetrical," (Wiegand, 132) containing an irrelevant "mass of detail." (Gwynn and Blotner, 46) In 1963, Warren French belittled the story as a "meandering torrent of words." (*J. D. Salinger*, 151).

"Seymour: An Introduction" has generally been condemned for its lack of structure and plot: "a piece of shapeless self-indulgence"; (Steiner, 83) "unabashed propaganda"; (French, *J. D. Salinger*, 155); and "as close to being an essay as a piece of fiction can." (Lundquist, 136) Current commentators still find "Seymour" unsatisfying, for "Seymour never finally comes to life. The book is a one [sic] long stutter and a fascinating failure" because "Seymour fragments and falls apart." (D'Ambrosio, 49)

Of course, not everyone disliked it. John Updike called "Raise High the Roof Beam, Carpenters" the best of Salinger's stories on the Glass family, "a magic and hilarious prose-poem with an enchanting end effect of mysterious clarity," (quoted in French, *Revisited*, 99) and Thomas Beller praised it as "an affecting and memorable piece of writing" because of "the diction, the syntax, the voice," even though the early pages are "almost suffocating." (141, 142)

Despite the bad reviews, *Raise High the Roof Beam, Carpenters and Seymour: An Introduction* was eagerly purchased, and by the sixth week of publication, it rose to first place on the *New York Times*' bestseller list. (Alexander, 227)

"Hapworth 16, 1924"

Published in the *New Yorker* on June 19, 1965, "Hapworth 16, 1924" is Salinger's longest story. Buddy tries to show the saintliness of his brother by reproducing a letter written by Seymour when he was a seven-year-old at Camp Simon Hapworth in Maine. The story consists of an introduction by Buddy, a description of camp life, some suggestions for the family, a request for a number of books, and a conclusion. Critics have agreed that this work has no plot but is, instead, "the long-winded, seemingly unedited ramblings of seven-year-old Seymour," (Alexander, 230) whose talking becomes "a pompous display of erudition that many commentators have found simply unreadable." (French, *Revisited,* 110) Even though Alsen carefully analyzes the structure of the story, proving that it has some form, critics still do not respond positively to the work. Seymour, rather than saintly, is seen as "revolting," "monstrous," and "hideous." (Lundquist, 148, 149) According to Edward Kosner of the *New York Post,* this story "was barely publishable. The material had gotten too precious, too inward. Salinger had become so preoccupied with his own concerns that it didn't translate into the outer world anymore." (quoted in Alexander, 230)

This story was almost published as a book in 1977 by Orchises Press. However, when a bad review of the original story was printed, the book was placed on hold indefinitely.

Conclusions on the Glass Family Stories

Although few critics have looked favorably on Salinger's last stories, some find them worthwhile. Sam S. Baskett enthusiastically writes that Salinger's Glass family stories "represent an exciting and original attempt to deal with the American experience," (61) and Alsen is touched by the Glass stories, stating that his "attitude . . . is not that of a detached critic but that of an undetached rhapsode." (xii) But overall, critics have harshly condemned Salinger's last stories because of their excessive style, rambling and almost plotless structure, and preachy religious messages. As French states, in his last publications, Salinger has allowed "the magician [to be] replaced by the lecturer." (*Revisited*, 99) As a result, French concludes, people are unwilling to read any more of Buddy/Salinger's works and therefore "one can only praise [Salinger's] decision to write for his own pleasure" but not publish his works. (*Revisited*, 116)

Chapter 5

Salinger's Place in Literature

J. D. SALINGER'S LITERARY REPUTATION rests primarily on one slim volume of work published more than a half century ago, *The Catcher in the Rye,* which enjoys a wide range of readers—professors, teachers, students, and the general public. Shortly after its publication, Salinger's novel was on the required reading lists at hundreds of high schools, colleges, and universities around the country. It "sold in the U.S. at the steady clip of 250,000 copies a year" (Dominic Smith, 641) and was on the *New York Times* bestseller list for thirty weeks, rising as high as the number four position. Within eight years Arthur Mizener declared that Salinger was "probably the most avidly read author of any serious pretensions of his generation." (202) The novel thrived abroad as well as in America. (Sublette, 216, 222; Silverberg, 11).

In spite of the book's popularity, its literary value is somewhat in dispute. Some critics have looked at *The Catcher in the Rye* with admiration, others with repulsion. This love/hate relationship began when the novel was first introduced to the world. Those attracted to the novel called it "strange and wonderful . . . an unusually brilliant first novel," (Nash Berger, quoted in Silverberg, 9) "engaging and believable," (Engle, 5) and "remarkable and absorbing." (Harrison Smith, 28) Those repulsed by the work viewed it as "a nightmarish medley of loneliness, bravado, and supineness . . . wholly repellent in its mingled vulgarity, naivete, and sly perversion." (Longstreth, 30)

Some critics consider *The Catcher in the Rye* merely a "minor classic," for it captured the mood and attitudes of its time. However, others find Salinger's novel a classic because of its continued popularity. Even today, Holden Caulfield's candor, humor, and alienation speak to readers. Furthermore, Salinger's command of the vernacular language, his effective use of symbolism, and his perceptive portrayal of adolescent experience have been admired by commentators.

Salinger's three collections of thirteen short stories are not as highly regarded or as avidly read as his novel. Two years after *The Catcher in the Rye* hit the market, *Nine Stories* appeared and it quickly became a bestseller. (Salzman, "Introduction," 7) However, as Paul Alexander pointed out, *Nine Stories* "surely would not have been as successful as it was" if *The Catcher in the Rye* had not been published. (25) The same is true of *Franny and Zooey* (1961), which also sold well largely because of *Catcher*'s popularity. (Alexander, 26) However, critics did not respond positively to the work, finding Salinger slipping as an artist because of his obsession with Eastern religions and his troubled personal life. *Raise High the Roof Beam, Carpenters and Seymour: An Introduction* (1963), and "Hapworth 16, 1924"(1965), reinforced their opinions that Salinger could no longer write anything of consequence. In fact, Salinger's last story is largely dismissed as a work of art.

Although the stories published in book form still remain popular with the same readers who admire *The Catcher in the Rye*, they "in no way demonstrate any advance or development in Salinger's narrative art. Seymour—their spiritual center—is rather hard to take." (Bloom, Introduction, 2)

In 1958, Frederick L. Gwynn and Joseph L. Blotner published *The Fiction of J. D. Salinger*, a critical review of Salinger's work. By the 1960s, a number of books began appearing on Salinger and his writings, most notably

Warren French's *J. D. Salinger* (1963), which was the first major study of Salinger, James E. Miller Jr.'s insightful *J. D. Salinger* (1965), and Kenneth Hamilton's *J. D. Salinger: A Critical Essay* (1967). From 1962 to 1966, five collections of Salinger criticism were published, and two special issues were devoted to Salinger's fiction.

However, with Salinger's retirement to the hills of Cornish in 1953 and his failure to publish after 1965, critical attention declined in the next decades. It was not until 1979 that a new major work was printed on Salinger, James Lundquist's *J. D. Salinger*. The 1980s brought four more works: by Eberhard Alsen, Warren French, Jack R. Sublette, and Ian Hamilton. In the 1990s only two important additions to Salinger scholarship appeared: Sanford Pinsker's analysis of *The Catcher in the Rye* and Paul Alexander's biography.

Critical collections suffered the same fate as the books. More than two decades passed before Harold Bloom gathered essays together in his 1987 book, *Modern Critical Interpretations: J. D. Salinger's* "The Catcher in the Rye," but these were largely old articles. However, in the early 1990s, two collections of largely new essays appeared, one by Joel Salzberg (1990), the other by Jack Salzman (1991). The early twenty-first century saw renewed interest in Salinger as collections of new essays were published by Harold Bloom (2000 and 2002), Kip Kotzen and Thomas Beller (2001), and J. P. Steed (2002). These works show the continued impact Salinger, and in particular, *The Catcher in the Rye*, has on readers.

Even though critical attention to Salinger's works waned, Salinger never lost his reading public, particularly the young readers of *The Catcher in the Rye*. As a result, censors have remained vigilant, for like the early reviewer T. Morris Longstreth, many find that the novel "is not fit for children to read" (30) because of its profanity, vulgarity, sexuality, immorality, and anti-American sentiments. The 1978 edition of *Banned Books: 387 B.C. to*

Mark David Chapman was arrested after assassinating famous former Beatle John Lennon. Chapman's bizarre misinterpretation of *The Catcher in the Rye* played a part in his action.

1978 A.D. reported that in *Catcher*'s first twenty-five years, "literally hundreds of attempts ha[d] been made to ban the book in schools throughout the United States." (Haight and Grannis, 92) As early as 1956, the National Office for Decent Literature objected to *The Catcher in the Rye*. (Whitfield, 82) In the following decades, citizens sought to keep the novel off the library shelves and out of high school reading lists in cities in California, Kentucky, Oklahoma, New York, Kansas, Massachusetts, Pennsylvania, Washington, Michigan, New Jersey, Ohio, Alabama, Montana, Florida, Wyoming, North Dakota, Indiana, Illinois, Iowa, Wisconsin, and New Hampshire. (Karolides, Bald, and Sova, 367–368)

Censors may have had some legitimate reasons for keeping the book out of the hands of impressionable readers. From the beginning, critics "condemned the book as insidious and corrupting," (Salzberg, "Introduction," 1) an assessment that, at least in part, is true, for Holden is so realistically portrayed that he has the "ability to . . . speak to gunmen, assassins such as John Hinckley and Mark David Chapman." (Walker, 80)

John Hinckley Jr. tried to assassinate President Ronald Reagan. Agents who arrested him found a copy of Salinger's novel in his coat pocket.

On Monday, December 8, 1980, Mark David Chapman shot his idol, John Lennon, in the back, holding the gun under a copy of *The Catcher in the Rye*. He then sat down on the curb and read Salinger's novel. Weeks later, Chapman stated: "My wish is for all of you to someday read *The Catcher in the Rye*, . . . for this extraordinary book holds many answers." (quoted in Alexander, 270) At his trial, Chapman's motives for killing Lennon were made clear: he believed that Lennon had become an insincere phony corrupted by commercialism. Therefore, to save his idol's innocence, he became a "catcher in the rye" by shooting him. When Chapman was explaining his action to television personality Barbara Walters years later, he told her that "before he went to kill John Lennon he had gone through a satanic ritual to make himself become Holden Caulfield . . . [so he could] cleanse the world of phony people." (Alexander, 271)

Four months after this murder, on March 30, 1981, John Hinckley Jr., desperately seeking the attention of movie actor Jodie Foster, waited in a crowd outside the Hilton

Hotel in Washington, D.C. When President Ronald Reagan appeared, he fired six times, wounding the president, his press secretary, a policeman, and a secret service agent. In the pockets of this man, who was described as "alienated" and "deranged," (quoted in Alexander, 271) was a well-worn copy of *The Catcher in the Rye*.

Several years later, another assassin carried a copy of *The Catcher in the Rye* as he took a life. On July 18, 1989, the sitcom actress Rebecca Schaeffer answered the door of her Los Angeles home and saw Robert John Bardo, a young ex-janitor with a history of mental illness. She had successfully ignored his advances in the past, but this night, he pointed a gun at her, shot her in the chest, and killed her. (Alexander, 290) Of course, it is not only murderers who are attracted by Holden, but they do illustrate the powerful hold Salinger's book has on those who feel alienated or who hate the world, which they view as phony or superficial.

On the good side, Salinger has inspired writers who "revived or re-imagined" Salinger "in a host of fictional and semi-fictional discourses." (Silverberg, 12) An early book incorporating *The Catcher in the Rye* is John Fowles' *The Collector* (1963), which includes a kidnapper who is seen as a type of Holden Caulfield. (When the book was adapted to a film, the section on Salinger's novel was abbreviated.) Another novel, W. P. Kinsella's 1982 best seller, *Shoeless Joe*, deals with the same theme as J. D. Salinger's works, the conflict between idealism and reality, and includes a character named Jerry Salinger, who moves out of his reclusive life in Cornish to reenter the world. When this book was adapted into the popular 1989 film *Field of Dreams*, most references to Salinger were removed, and, for legal reasons, Salinger's character's name was changed to Terence Mann. (Walker, 82) John Guare's 1990 play, *Six Degrees of Separation*, and the 1993 film adaptation directed by Fred Schepisi, have a main character who claims to be writing his Harvard thesis on

The Catcher in the Rye and creates a Salinger-like text of his imaginary life. Two other works in this decade refer to Salinger's novel. The 1991 film *Guilty by Suspicion* features a screenwriter who burns Salinger's novel after the House Un-American Activities Committee alleged that the book promoted communism. And Eve Horowitz's 1992 novel *Plain Jane* includes a young female narrator who identifies with Holden Caulfield. (52, 200, 230) (Whitfield, 86)

In addition to books and films, television sitcoms in the 1990s, in particular "Mad About You" and "The Single Guy," used Salinger's name and presence. (Silverberg, 12)

Some authors, although not specifically referring to Salinger or *The Catcher in the Rye*, have also been influenced by him. Mark Silverberg suggests that Salinger's self-imposed exile may have been a model for Don DeLillo's "reclusive writer" in *Mao II* (1991). (12) Matt Evertson notes that Cormac McCarthy's coming-of-age novel, *All the Pretty Horses* (1992), uses a protagonist similar to Holden Caulfield—a sixteen-year-old who wants to escape the adult world of materialism and selfishness. In addition, this novel, like *The Catcher in the Rye*, explores the themes of innocence and youth, love and death. (102–104)

All of these literary works show how deeply Salinger has influenced and inspired his readers. Jack Salzman is accurate that "despite [Salinger's] dismissal by some critics, his failure to publish anything [since 1965], and the competing popularity of such writers as Toni Morrison, Thomas Pynchon, and Kurt Vonnegut Jr., *The Catcher in the Rye* retains a remarkable hold on our imagination." ("Introduction," 16)

It is not only the novel that has provided fodder for criticism, speculation, and controversy, but also Salinger who has made himself into a myth, a type of Holden Caulfield who dared to leave the phony world and become a hermit in the hills of Cornish, New Hampshire. Because his continued isolation has sparked much speculation about his life and his writing, reporters, biographers, and fans have stalked the inaccessible writer to try to glean information about him. By cutting himself off from the world, Salinger, as biographer Paul Alexander asserts, ensures that any contact he makes will be a media event. Therefore very mundane, everyday things are covered by the press, such as a picture in *Time* of the reclusive author going to the grocery store and a notice in *Newsweek* of his attendance at an army friend's retirement party. (Alexander, 26) The myth of the inspired writer who lives an idyllic, pastoral life happily writing books for his own pleasure has largely evaporated with the publications of two works about the intimate details of Salinger's life since his move to Cornish. His former mistress, Joyce Maynard, published *At Home in the World: A Memoir* in 1998, and his daughter, Margaret Ann (Peggy) Salinger, published *Dream Catcher: A Memoir* in 2000.

In spite of the unflattering portraits of Salinger, his books, especially *The Catcher in the Rye*, remain popular. In the first ten years it was on the market, it sold 3.5 million copies in the United States; by 1981, 10 million had been sold, and by 1996, 15 million. (Alexander, 26) Salinger's other three books, *Nine Stories*, *Franny and Zooey*, and *Raise High the Roof Beam, Carpenters and Seymour: An Introduction*, have also sold millions of copies. (Alexander, 302) With the profits from these four books, Salinger was able to retire and live a life of relative ease for almost half a century.

Why *The Catcher in the Rye* remains popular has been the subject of speculation for decades, but, clearly, Holden Caulfield resonated with the young people of the 1950s, and he has continued to appeal to later generations. George Steiner offers four possible reasons that the novel is attractive to young people. First, Salinger uses young protagonists and "the young like to read about the young." Second, "Salinger writes briefly," and young people like to read short works. Third, Salinger's works are simple: "He demands of his readers nothing in the way of literary or political interest." And fourth, Salinger makes inexperienced readers feel good about themselves: "Salinger flatters the very ignorance and moral shallowness of his young readers" treating "formal ignorancc, political apathy, and a vague tristesse [as] positive virtues." (83)

Although these negative reasons can account for some of the novel's popularity, they do not provide the total picture. Readers like the novel because it is technically very good. Salinger is very skilled in descriptions, and he has "a first-rate ear for the mannerisms of American speech, particularly those peculiar to the young." (Swados, 120) In addition, readers relate to Holden because Salinger incorporates the universal themes of conformity, alienation, loneliness, community, family, friendship, and love into his work. Adding to the popularity of the novel is the mystique surrounding the reclusive, silent writer.

Although Salinger's novel has continued to be popular, not many would agree with the statement made by James E. Miller Jr. in 1965 that Salinger deserves "the preeminent position" in post World War II American fiction. (45) Of his four published books, only one is considered great—*The Catcher in the Rye*. In it, "Salinger's voice was as striking as any writer's of our time." (Salzman, "Introduction," 18) And on it rests Salinger's legacy. It is Holden Caulfield, and no other character, who "constitutes Salinger's achievement." (Bloom, "Introduction," 2) And this achievement is quite impressive. J. P. Steed argues that in 1950s America, "Holden Caulfield—do we dare say single-handedly?—(re)defined the identity of the American teenagers and subsequently reconstructed the identity of Americans." ("Introduction," 3) Since that decade, Holden has permeated American culture, and more than fifty years later "the novel's power still lives on." (Steed, "Introduction," 5) Mark Silverberg accurately sums up Salinger's appeal and place in literature: "That the author of one novel and several dozen stories has seized and compelled our collective imagination for so long is testament as much to our need for the kind of story he tells as it is to Salinger's undeniable talent for providing this story." (28)

Chronology

1919

January 1: Jerome David Salinger (nicknamed Salinger) is born in New York City, son of Sol and Miriam Jillich Salinger, and brother of Doris. Lives in northern Harlem.

Family moves to Jewish Upper West Side in New York City.

1920–1928

Family moves three times.

1924–1932

Attends Upper West Side (New York City) public schools (grades 1–8), with a majority of Jewish classmates.

1930

Summer: Voted "most popular actor" at Camp Wigwam, Harrison, Maine.

1932

Family moves to Park Avenue, a wealthy White Anglo-Saxon Protestant (WASP) neighborhood in Upper East Side, New York City.

Enrolls as a high school freshman in McBurney School, a private Young Men's Christian Association movement school in Manhattan.

1933

January: Has bar mitzvah.

Discovers he is only half Jewish.

1934

Spring: Flunks out of McBurney School.

Summer: Takes classes at the Manhasset School in effort to make up poor grades.

Fall: Enrolls as high school junior in Valley Forge Military Academy, Wayne, Pennsylvania.

1935

Becomes literary editor of *Crossed Sabres*, the school yearbook.

1936

June: Graduates from Valley Forge Military Academy.

Fall: Attends New York University's (NYU) Washington Square College.

1937

Spring: Drops out of NYU.

Works as entertainment director on a cruise ship, the Swedish liner *MS Kungsholm*.

Fall: Travels to Vienna, Austria, and Bydgoszcz, Poland (with visits to Paris and London) for five months to learn his father's meat and cheese import business.

1938

Early Spring: Returns to United States.

Fall: Enrolls as a freshman at Ursinus College in Collegeville, Pennsylvania.

Writes column, "The Skipped Diploma," for *Ursinus Weekly.*

Drops out of school after attending for a semester; lives with parents.

1939

Spring: Audits Whit Burnett's short-story writing class at Columbia University; writes no stories.

Fall: Audits Burnett's class at Columbia University once more; produces three stories.

1940

March–April: Publishes "The Young Folks" in Burnett's *Story,* his first published story.

Summer: Travels to Cape Cod and Canada.

September: Returns to New York City and lives with parents.

September 6: Decides to use initials "J. D." instead of "Jerome" in his publications.

December: Publishes "Go See Eddie" in the *University of Kansas City Review.*

1941

July 12: Publishes "The Hang of It" (renamed "A Short Story Complete on This Page") in *Collier's.*

Summer: Begins dating Oona O'Neill, age sixteen, Eugene O'Neill's daughter.
September: Publishes "The Heart of a Broken Story" in *Esquire*.
Sells first story about Holden Caulfield, "Slight Rebellion Off Madison," to the *New Yorker*, which is not printed until 1946.
Classified 1-B by Selective Service.
December 7: Pearl Harbor attacked; United States enters World War II.

1942
April 27: Drafted into the U.S. Army; attends Officers, First Sergeants, and Instructors School of the Signal Corps at Fort Monmouth, New Jersey.
June: Applies and is accepted for Officer Training School, but not called up.
July: Assigned to instructor's job with Army Aviation Cadets at U.S. Army Air Force Basic Flying School in Bainbridge, Georgia.
September–October: Publishes "The Long Debut of Lois Taggett" in *Story*.
Fall: Oona O'Neill ends romance and later marries fifty-four-year-old Charlie Chaplin.
December 12: Publishes "Personal Notes of an Infantryman" in *Collier's*.

1943
Attains rank of staff sergeant and is stationed near Nashville, Tennessee.
Transferred to work in public relations at Patterson Field in Fairfield, Ohio.
July 17: Publishes "The Varioni Brothers" in the *Saturday Evening Post*.
October: Transferred to Fort Holabird, Maryland, to train as a special agent for the Army Counterintelligence Corps.

1944
February 26: Publishes "Both Parties Concerned" in the *Saturday Evening Post;* is upset his title, "Wake Me When It Thunders," has been changed.
March: Receives Counterintelligence training at Tiverton, Devon, England.
April 15: Publishes "Soft Boiled Sergeant" in the *Saturday Evening Post;* is upset his title, "Death of a Dogface," has been changed.
June 6: Lands with 4th Army Division at Utah Beach on D-day invasion of Normandy.

June–August: Fights with Twelfth Infantry Regiment from Utah Beach to Cherbourg to Paris.
July 15: Publishes "The Last Day of the Last Furlough" in the *Saturday Evening Post.*
August: Meets Ernest Hemingway in Paris.
September–December: Fights in some of the worst battles of World War II with the Twelfth Infantry Regiment.
November–December: Publishes "Once a Week Won't Kill You" in *Story.*

1945
January–May: Continues fighting with the 12th Infantry Regiment in Germany (fights in five campaigns in World War II).
March–April: Publishes "Elaine" in *Story.*
March 31: Publishes "A Boy in France" in the *Saturday Evening Post.*
May 7: VE-day (Victory in Europe)
May, June, or July: Suffers a nervous breakdown and is hospitalized in Nuremberg; fears he will receive a psychiatric discharge from army.
July 27: Writes letter of adulation to Ernest Hemingway.
August: Released from hospital.
September or October: Marries Sylvia, a German doctor.
October: Publishes "This Sandwich Has No Mayonnaise" in *Esquire.*
November: Discharged from army. Signs a six month civilian contract with Department of Defense.
December: Lives with wife in Gunzenhausen, Germany.
December 1: Publishes "The Stranger" in *Collier's.*
December 22: Publishes "I'm Crazy" in *Collier's*, his first story about Holden Caulfield.

1946
May: Returns to United States with wife, Sylvia, and lives with parents.
June 13: Terminates marriage to Sylvia, who returns to Europe; lives with parents on Park Avenue.
Submits original version of *The Catcher in the Rye* to the *New Yorker* as a ninety page novella; withdraws the manuscript.
December 21: Publishes "Slight Rebellion Off Madison" in the *New Yorker,* his first story in this magazine.

1947
January: Moves to a garage apartment in Tarrytown, New York.
May: Publishes "A Young Girl in 1941 with No Waist at All" in *Mademoiselle.*
Fall (probably): Moves to a barn studio in Stamford, Connecticut.
December: Publishes "The Inverted Forest" in *Cosmopolitan.*

1948
January 31: Publishes "A Perfect Day for Bananafish" in the *New Yorker;* appears in *55 Short Stories 1940–50, from* the New Yorker.
February: Publishes "A Girl I Knew" in *Good Housekeeping* but is upset his title, "Wien, Wien," has been changed.
Signs contract with the *New Yorker,* a recognition that he is a serious creative writer.
March 20: Publishes "Uncle Wiggily in Connecticut" in the *New Yorker.*
June 5: Publishes "Just Before the War with the Eskimos" in the *New Yorker.*
September: Publishes "Blue Melody" in *Cosmopolitan,* but is upset his title, "Scratchy Needle on a Phonograph Record," has been changed.

1949
March 19: Publishes "The Laughing Man" in the *New Yorker.*
April: Publishes "Down at the Dinghy" in *Harper's* magazine.
Gives one-day lecture to short-story class at Sarah Lawrence College.
Fall: Moves to rented house in Westport, Connecticut.

1950s
Begins formal study of Eastern religion and philosophy; embraces Zen Buddhism and Vedanta Hinduism, on and off, and L. Ron Hubbard's Scientology (called Dianetics), and the works of Edgar Cayce.

1950
January 21: Film version of "Uncle Wiggily in Connecticut," *My Foolish Heart*, starring Susan Hayward and Dana Andrews, is released by Samuel Goldwyn; Salinger is upset with the changes to his story and refuses to sell screen or television rights to any of his other works.

April 8: Publishes "For Esmé—with Love and Squalor" in the *New Yorker;* selected by Martha Foley as one of the distinguished short stories published in American magazines in 1950 and published in *Prize Stories of 1950.*
Fall: Studies Eastern religions.
Fall: Meets Claire Douglas, a sixteen-year-old high school senior, and begins corresponding with her.

1951
March: Becomes friends with British publisher Hamish Hamilton and his wife.
Summer: Begins dating Claire Douglas.
Summer: Travels to British Isles to avoid publicity for *The Catcher in the Rye.*
July 14: Publishes "Pretty Mouth and Green My Eyes" in the *New Yorker.*
July 16: *The Catcher in the Rye* is published by Little, Brown and Company; selected for Book-of-the-Month Club.
August: Rents an apartment (the black apartment) at 300 East Fifty-Seventh Street, New York City.

1952
January: Becomes friends with William Shawn, new editor of the *New Yorker.*
March–June: Visits Florida and Mexico.
Selected for one of three Distinguished Alumni of the Year awards at Valley Forge Military Academy.
May: Publishes "De Daumier-Smith's Blue Period" in London's *World Review.*

1953
January 1: Buys a cottage on ninety acres; moves to Cornish, New Hampshire, and becomes a recluse.
January 31: Publishes "Teddy" in the *New Yorker.*
Winter: Asks Claire Douglas, age nineteen, to drop out of Radcliffe College and live with him; she refuses.
Disappears (probably travels to Europe).
Spring: Claire marries a Harvard Business School graduate.
April 6: *Nine Stories* is published by Little, Brown.

November: Interviewed by Shirlie Blaney for the Windsor (VT) High School page that appeared monthly in the *Claremont* (New Hampshire) *Daily Eagle*. Offended when interview is printed on *Daily Eagle* editorial page, November 13.

1954
Embraces Kriya yoga (through 1955).
Claire's marriage is annulled.
Summer: Begins courting Claire once more.
Fall: Claire moves in with Salinger but attends Radcliffe.

1955
Embraces Christian Science religion (on and off to present).
January 29: Publishes "Franny" in the *New Yorker.*
February 17: Marries Claire Douglas, who quits Radcliffe four months before graduation.
November 19: Publishes "Raise High the Roof Beam, Carpenters" in the *New Yorker*.
December 10: Daughter, Margaret Ann (called Peggy), is born.

1956
Builds cabin (called Green House) in forest and spends time writing there.

1957
Winter: Claire leaves with baby and lives in New York City.
May 4: Publishes "Zooey" in the *New Yorker*.
Summer: Claire and baby return to Cornish to live with Salinger.

1959
June 6: Publishes "Seymour: An Introduction" in the *New Yorker.*

1960s
Embraces homeopathy and acupuncture (through the present).

1960
February 13: Son, Matthew Robert, is born.

1961
September 14: *Franny and Zooey* published by Little, Brown.

September 15: Appears on cover of *Time* magazine.
Fall: Renovates and enlarges house; has private apartment over the garage.

1963
January 28: *Raise High the Roof Beam, Carpenters and Seymour: An Introduction* published by Little, Brown.

1965
June 19: Publishes "Hapworth 16, 1924," his most recent published story, in the *New Yorker.*

1966
September 9: Claire files for divorce.
Embraces macrobiotics (until the end of divorce from Claire).
Buys additional 475 acres; builds a new house for himself.

1967
October 3: Divorce granted to Claire Salinger.
1968 Travels with children to England and Scotland to meet teenage pen pal.
1970
Spring: Father, Sol Salinger, dies.

1971
Mother, Miriam Jillich Salinger, dies.

1972
April 25: Begins corresponding with Joyce Maynard, an eighteen-year-old freshman at Yale.
September: Joyce Maynard quits college and moves in with Salinger.

1973
March: Breaks up with Joyce Maynard.

1974
Takes legal action to suppress the unauthorized *Complete Uncollected Short Stories of J. D. Salinger,* published in two volumes in Berkeley, California.

1970s and 1980s:
Lives with a variety of young women.

1977 or 1978:
Meets the teenager, Colleen O'Neill, and begins corresponding with her.

1980
Continues corresponding with Colleen, who marries a man named Mike.

1981
Begins romance with Elaine Joyce, a thirty-six-year-old actress.

1983
Thanksgiving: Colleen leaves husband and son; moves in with Salinger.
Breaks up with Elaine Joyce.

1986
Suit against San Francisco booksellers over pirated collection of short stories settled in Salinger's favor.
September: Sues biographer Ian Hamilton and publisher Random House for unauthorized use of his unpublished correspondence in *J. D. Salinger: A Writing Life.*
November 5: Loses his suit against Ian Hamilton.
December 3: Appeals court decision in favor of Ian Hamilton.

1987
January 29: Wins court appeal and blocks Ian Hamilton from publishing biography.
January: Joins other *New Yorker* contributors in protest against replacement of editor William Shawn by new publishers.
March 8: Son Matthew (Matt) stars in CBS telefilm *Deadly Deception.*
September 5: Lawyers for Random House appeal to U.S. Supreme Court.
October 5: Court denies Random House's petition, blocking publication of Hamilton's *J. D. Salinger: A Writing Life.*

1988
February 2: Kevin Sim's documentary, *The Man Who Shot John Lennon*, shown on British TV.

February 9: PBS "Frontline" dramatized the way Mark David Chapman misused *The Catcher in the Rye* as his incentive to shoot John Lennon.
Ian Hamilton's rewritten biography, *In Search of J. D. Salinger,* published.

Late 1980s (or early 1990s) Marries Colleen O'Neill, his third wife.

1992
House catches on fire; people discover young woman living with Salinger is his wife.

1998
Hapworth 16, 1924, almost published as a book by Orchises Press.
Joyce Maynard's book on her affair with Salinger, *At Home in the World: A Memoir*, published.

2000
Margaret A. Salinger's book, *Dream Catcher: A Memoir*, published.

Works

Books

1951 *The Catcher in the Rye*
1953 *Nine Stories*
1961 *Franny and Zooey*
1963 *Raise High the Roof Beam, Carpenters and Seymour: An Introduction*
1974 *The Complete Uncollected Short Stories of J. D. Salinger*, 2 volumes (privately published).

Short Stories

1940 "The Young Folks"
"Go See Eddie"
1941 "The Hang of It"
"The Heart of a Broken Story"
1942 "The Long Debut of Lois Taggett"
"Personal Notes of an Infantryman"
1943 "The Varioni Brothers"
1944 "Both Parties Concerned"
"Soft-Boiled Sergeant"
"Last Day of the Last Furlough"
"Once a Week Won't Kill You"
1945 "Elaine"
"A Boy in France"
"This Sandwich Has No Mayonnaise"
"The Stranger"
"I'm Crazy"
1946 "A Slight Rebellion off Madison"
1947 "A Young Girl in 1941 with No Waist at All"
"The Inverted Forest"
1948 "A Perfect Day for Bananafish"
"A Girl I Knew"
"Uncle Wiggily in Connecticut"
"Just Before the War with the Eskimos"
"Blue Melody"

1949 "The Laughing Man"
"Down at the Dinghy"
1950 "For Esmé—with Love and Squalor"
1951 "Pretty Mouth and Green My Eyes"
1952 "De Daumier-Smith's Blue Period"
1953 "Teddy"
1955 "Franny"
"Raise High the Roof Beam, Carpenters"
1957 "Zooey"
1959 "Seymour: An Introduction"
1965 "Hapworth 16, 1924"

Miscellaneous Prose

1955 "Man-Forsaken Man"
1975 "Epilogue: A Salute to Whit Burnett, 1899–1972"

Unpublished Stories in *Story* Magazine Archives at Columbia University

"The Children's Echelon"
"The Last and Best of the Peter Pans"
"The Magic Foxhole"
"The Ocean Full of Bowling Balls"
"Two Lonely Men"

Filmography and Other Recordings

Adaptations of J. D. Salinger's Works

1949 *My Foolish Heart*. A motion picture based on "Uncle Wiggily in Connecticut." Directed by Mark Robson. Starring Susan Hayward and Dana Andrews. Samuel Goldwyn Studio.

1984 *Fragmento*. A short drama produced in Mexico in Spanish. Directed by Miguel Mora. Writing credits given to Miguel Mora and J. D. Salinger.

1995 *Pari*. An unauthorized adaptation of *Franny and Zooey*. Produced in Iran in Farsi. Directed by Dariush Mehrjui. Written by Dariush Mehrjui and J. D. Salinger. Starring Niki Karimi and Khosro Shakibai.

Films with References to J. D. Salinger or His Works

1965 *The Collector*. Based on John Fowles' novel *The Collector*. Includes a discussion of *The Catcher in the Rye*. Directed by William Wyler. Starring Terence Stamp and Samantha Eggar. Columbia Pictures.

1989 *Field of Dreams*. Based on W. P. Kinsella's novel *Shoeless Joe*, has a character named "Jerry Salinger," changed to "Terence Mann" in the film for legal reasons. Directed by Phil Alden Robinson. Starring Kevin Costner and Amy Madigan. Universal Pictures.

1990 *Guilty By Suspicion*. Contains a book-burning scene in which *The Catcher in the Rye* is burned for promoting communism. Directed by Irwin Winkler. Starring Robert De Niro, Annette Bening, George Wendt, Patricia Wettig, and Sam Wanamaker. Warner Brothers.

1993 *Six Degrees of Separation*. Based on John Guare's play *Six Degrees of Separation*. Has a main character who is writing about *The Catcher in the Rye*. Directed by Fred Schepisi. Starring Stockard Channing, Will Smith, Donald Sutherland, and Ian McKellen. MGM/United Artists Studios.

Film and Recording About J. D. Salinger

1998 *At Home in the World: A Memoir* by Joyce Maynard (abridged). An audiocassette read by the author. Published by Soudeluz Audio Publishing. Relates an account of the author's 1972 affair with Salinger.

1999 *J. D. Salinger Doesn't Want to Talk*. Film for the Humanities. Available in VHS and DVD.

Notes

Chapter 1

p. 11, par. 2, Margaret Salinger. *Dream Catcher: A Memoir.* New York: Washington Square Press, 2000, pp. 20–21.

p. 13, par. 1, Ibid., pp. 16–17.

p. 13, par. 3, Ibid., p. 29.

p. 14, par. 1, Professor Jacob R. Marcus of the Hebrew Union College-Jewish Institute of Religion explains that in spite of the anti-Semitism of the 1920s, "an integrated, united, local American Jewish community" looked out for the welfare of its people (205). But a person of mixed heritage, as Doris and J. D. Salinger learned, lost the support of the Jewish community. *See* Jacob R. Marcus. *Studies in American Jewish History.* (Cincinnati: Hebrew Union College Press), 1969, p. 205.

p. 14, par. 3, Although some biographers think Sol enrolled his son in a military school to force him to "shape up," Salinger's daughter is convinced that her father went willingly, noting that her grandmother would never force Salinger to do anything against his will, nor would she let her husband make him do anything. (Margaret Salinger, pp. 32–33)

p. 15, par. 1, For further information on Salinger's life at Valley Forge, see the following works: Ian Hamilton. *In Search of J. D. Salinger: A Biography.* (New York: Vintage Books, 1989), pp. 25–30; Warren French. *J. D. Salinger.* (New York: Twayne, 1963), p. 22; Warren French. *J. D. Salinger, Revisited.* (Boston: Twayne, 1988), p. 2.

p. 15, par. 2, Paul Alexander. *Salinger: A Biography.* (Los Angeles: Renaissance Books, 1999), pp. 40–42.

p. 15, par. 4, Biographer Ian Hamilton questions why Salinger did not apply to one of the Ivy League schools, such as Harvard or Yale (Hamilton, p. 37). But Salinger would have had a hard time being accepted because of his poor grades and because these schools rarely accepted Jewish students or teachers. Salinger's daughter explains that her father despised Ivy League schools because they were very anti-Semitic in the 1930s. This is probably the primary reason Salinger wrote with disdain about Ivy Leaguers, such as Lane Coutell in "Franny." For further information about Salinger's views on Ivy League schools, *see* Margaret Salinger, pp. 35–39; and Norma Jean Lutz. "Biography of J. D. Salinger," in *Bloom's*

BioCritiques: J. D. Salinger, ed. Harold Bloom. (Philadelphia: Chelsea House, 2002), p. 11.

p. 15, par 4, Salinger made it clear that he was merely passing time at college. In a satiric column for the college newspaper, the *Ursinus Weekly*, he stated: "Once there was a young man who was tired of trying to grow a moustache. This same young man did not want to go to work for his Daddykins—or any other unreasonable man. So the young man went back to college." (quoted in Ian Hamilton, p. 46)

p. 17, par. 3, Joyce Maynard writes that Salinger thought he could make a lot of money because he considered himself more talented than F. Scott Fitzgerald, Ring Lardner, and Ernest Hemingway. (Joyce Maynard. *At Home in the World: A Memoir.* New York: Picador, 1998, p. 333.)

p. 18, par. 1, On July 12, 1941, *Collier's* printed "The Hang of It," a very short story, which it renamed "A Short Story Complete on This Page," and in September *Esquire* carried his satirical "Heart of a Broken Story." Salinger was ecstatic when "Slight Rebellion Off Madison," his first story about Holden Caulfield, was purchased by the elite *New Yorker*, but his joy turned to disappointment when the editors decided not to print it after the bombing of Pearl Harbor; it finally appeared in 1946.

p. 19, par. 1, After reporting to Fort Dix, New Jersey, Private Salinger attended Officers, First Sergeants, and Instructors School of the Signal Corps at Fort Monmouth, New Jersey. He applied for Officer Candidate School, and, although he was accepted, he was not called. In July, he was assigned to an instructor's job with the Army Aviation Cadets at U.S. Army Air Force Basic Flying School at Bainbridge, Georgia. By 1943, Salinger, now a staff sergeant, was stationed near Nashville, Tennessee, and because of his writing fame, was later transferred to work in public relations at Patterson Field in Fairfield, Ohio. In October, he was selected to be a special agent for counterintelligence and began training at Fort Holabird, Maryland.

p. 19, par. 1, In 1942, two stories appeared: *Story* printed "The Long Debut of Lois Taggett," which Salinger had written before he joined the army, and *Collier's* published "Personal Notes of an Infantryman," his first army story. After the well-paying and popular *Saturday Evening Post* carried "The Varioni Brothers" in 1943, Salinger found a good market for his stories. The next year *Saturday Evening Post* published three of his stories dealing with war and the military: "Wake Me When It Thunders", retitled "Both Parties Concerned," (February 26); "Death of a Dogface," retitled "Soft Boiled Sergeant" (April 15); and "The Last Day of the Last

Furlough" (July 15). Salinger was angry that the titles of the first two stories were changed, and this also caused him to become distrustful of editors. At the close of the year, "Once a Week Won't Kill You" appeared in *Story.*

p. 19, par. 4, On D-day, twenty-five-year-old Salinger and his comrades were transported across the English Channel to Utah Beach. But the boats, impeded by strong currents, mines, and sandbars, could not get the men to shore. Nauseated from the pitching waves, they were forced to jump into waist-deep water. Carrying heavy equipment, they waded two hundred feet to shore while under heavy fire from German gunmen. Once they reached the shore, Salinger's division fought on an open beach. Pushing inland, the Twelfth Infantry trudged through lands flooded by the Germans, trying to keep from drowning in the muddy water that was waist-deep in some places, but over the men's heads in the treacherous irrigation ditches. By the end of the day, Utah Beach was secured. For further information about D-day events, see the following works: Stephen E. Ambrose. *D-Day, June 6, 1944: The Climactic Battle of World War II.* (New York: Simon and Schuster, 1994); Stephen E. Ambrose. *The Victors: Eisenhower and His Boys: The Men of World War II.* (New York: Simon and Schuster, 1998), pp. 108–116; and Gerden Johnson. *History of the Twelfth Infantry Regiment in World War II.* (Boston: 4th Division Association, 1947), pp. 57–60.

p. 20, par. 1, Beginning on June 7, those in Salinger's division who survived Utah Beach began an excruciating drive to the port town of Cherbourg, Normandy, engaging in one of the most intense battles of World War II, the Battle of the Hedgerows. The Norman hedgerows, which lined the roads, were formed of cementlike banks of earth three to seven feet high and topped with thickets and trees that arched over the roads. As the Americans moved down the sunken, hedge-lined roads, the Nazis were lying in wait to ambush them. Charging the entrenched Nazis with bayonets while dodging bullets, mortars, and tank guns, the Americans gallantly struggled to reach Cherbourg, in what Colonel Johnson called "a miracle of human endurance." (Johnson, 58) As they advanced, Salinger's job as a counterintelligence agent was to destroy the enemy's lines of communications by cutting telephone lines and seizing post offices in the fallen towns. His next task was to interrogate the masses of prisoners, looking for German collaborators and army deserters wearing civilian clothes. (Lutz, 5) Once in Cherbourg, Salinger's unit spent a week engaging in hand-to-hand combat, going from building to building as they cleared the Nazis out of the city. By June 27, Cherbourg was in Allied hands, but Salinger's infantry had suffered many casualties. For more on hedgerow fighting and the conquering of Cherbourg, see the following works: Johnson, pp. 58–120; Ambrose, *D-Day,* p. 220; Ambrose, *Victors,* pp. 188–217; Stephen Ambrose. *Band of Brothers: E Company, 506th Regiment, 101st Airborne from Normandy to Hitler's Eagle's Nest.* (New York: Simon and Schuster, 2001), p. 91; and Stephen E. Ambrose. *Citizen Soldiers: The U. S. Army from the Normandy Beaches to the Bulge to the Surrender of Germany, June 7, 1944–May 7, 1945.* (New York: Simon and Schuster, 1997), pp. 19–51.

p. 20, par. 2, Immediately after securing Cherbourg, Salinger and his unit were deployed to Paris, again fighting their way through the treacherous Norman hedgerows in what Colonel Johnson says was "hedgerow fighting at its worst" (123). Inching forward, Salinger's division gained only a few hundred yards. Finally, on July 17, the Cotentin Peninsula was liberated, and Salinger's Twelfth Infantry got to shower and change their clothes for the first time since leaving England on June 4 (Johnson, 132). Advancing south for the next weeks, Col. Johnson reports the fighting "was more of the same—more hedgerows, more flooded rivers, more German snipers, more suffering and weariness" (136). August 9–12, Col. Johnson says, was "the fiercest, bloodiest contest in the entire history of the 12th Infantry," which battled against Hitler's most fanatical troops at bloody Mortain (157). Finally out of the hedgerows, Salinger's Twelfth Infantry began traveling the 165 miles of muddy, treacherous roads to Paris. For further information on the fighting in the Cotentin Peninsula, see Ambrose, *Victors,* pp. 188–217.

p. 20, par. 2, The Parisians covered their vehicles with flowers, showered the men with fruit and wine, and greeted them with kisses, hugs, and handshakes. See Johnson, p. 171.

p. 21, par. 1, Salinger's unit spent September and October driving the Germans back toward Germany, reaching the Hürtgen Forest, a 50-square-mile, densely wooded area on the German-Belgian border, in November. According to one of the sergeants in Salinger's division, the dark forest was an "eerie place to fight. You can't get protection. You can't see. You can't get fields of fire. . . . You can scarcely walk. Everybody is cold and wet, and the mixture of cold rain and sleet keeps falling." (Ambrose, *Victors*, 266) In the ice-lined foxholes, the GIs had few blankets to keep themselves warm and, worse yet, suffered from trench foot. As their toenails fell out and their feet turned from white to purple to black, the infected men were unable to walk. Many lost their toes, their feet, or, if gangrene set in, their entire lower legs. (Ambrose, *Victors*, 301) After a month of violent fighting, Salinger's Twelfth Infantry had possession of its portion of the Hürtgen Forest, but the toll was high. A total of 1,439 men died in battle and another 1,024 from other means, usually from freezing. In addition to the physical casualties, the men suffered lifelong emotional and psychological scars. As Stephen E. Ambrose, who interviewed thousands of veterans, explained, "There were no unwounded foxhole veterans." (*Victors*, 307) For further information on the battle at Hürtgen Forest, see Ambrose, *Victors,* pp. 266–321.

p. 21, par. 2, The Battle of the Bulge was a horrific battle fought from December 16, 1944 to January 25, 1945. When three German armies, trying to break through to the sea, surprised the Americans at Ardennes Forest on the Germany-Belgium/Luxembourg border, Salinger's regiment was charged with defending five road junctions to prevent the Germans from moving their equipment and troops up to the main battle lines. For further information on the Battle of the Bulge, *see* Johnson, pp. 243–262.

p. 21, par. 4, Salinger published five stories in 1945: "A Boy in France" in the *Saturday Evening Post* on March 31, "Elaine" in *Story* in March–April, "This Sandwich Has No Mayonnaise" in *Esquire* in October, "The Stranger" in *Collier's* on December 1, and "I'm Crazy" in *Collier's* on December 22. Some material from "I'm Crazy" is included in *The Catcher in the Rye.*

p. 22, par. 2, From his hospital bed, Salinger wrote a letter to Ernest Hemingway. According to Carlos Baker, Hemingway's biographer, Salinger informed the older writer that he continued to write and was currently working on a play about a boy and his sister, Holden and Phoebe Caulfield. Still interested in becoming an actor, he told Hemingway he planned to play the part of Holden. (Carlos Baker. *Ernest Hemingway: A Life Story.* New York: Scribners, 1969, p. 889.)

p. 24, par. 2, Peggy relates that decades after Salinger's divorce from Sylvia, in 1972, he received an envelope from her, which he dumped in the garbage without opening it because, as he told Peggy, when "he's finished with a person, he was through with them." (Margaret Salinger, p. 359)

p. 24, par. 3, Old friends fondly remember him from his Greenwich Village days as a young man who refused to accept money from his parents while trying to make a living with his writing; who was warm, but distant, to his parents; who wore tweed jackets with elbow patches of leather; and who loved dogs. *See* Henry Anatole Grunwald. "The Invisible Man: A Biographical Collage," in *Salinger: A Critical and Personal Portrait,* ed. Henry Anatole Grunwald. (New York: Harper and Row, 1962), p. 19. A fellow writer, A. E. Hotchner, remembers being amazed at his friend's "complete confidence in his destiny as a writer—a writer he was and a writer he would always be, and what's more, an important writer." (quoted in Lutz, p. 20)

p. 24, par. 4, The stories Salinger sold in 1947 were "A Young Girl in 1941 with No Waist at All," a story based on his time as an entertainment director on the cruise ship, to *Mademoiselle,* and "The Inverted Forest" to *Cosmopolitan.*

p. 25, par. 2, In 1948, the *New Yorker* published "A Perfect Day for Bananafish" on January 31, "Uncle Wiggily in Connecticut" on March 20, and "Just Before the War with the Eskimos" on June 5. *Good Housekeeping* carried "A Girl I Knew" (titled "Wien, Wien" by Salinger) in February, and *Cosmopolitan* printed "Blue Melody" (titled "Scratchy Needle on a Phonograph Record" by Salinger) in September.

p. 25, par. 3, In 1949, two stories appeared: "The Laughing Man" in the *New Yorker* and "Down at the Dinghy" in *Harper's Magazine.*

p. 26, par. 1, Critic Warren French feels that the release of this movie, which Salinger so despised, probably provided the final blow to Salinger's theatrical aspirations. French, *Salinger Revisited,* p. 5.

page 26, par. 3, "For Esmé—with Love and Squalor" appeared in 1950 and "Pretty Mouth and Green My Eyes," in 1951, both in the *New Yorker.*

p. 26, par. 3, British publisher Roger Machell called Salinger "perhaps the most brilliant but certainly by far the nuttiest author" he knew, adding that the author "has a profound hatred of all publishers." (quoted in Lutz, p. 31)

p. 27, par. 3, Eberhard Alsen explains that in the 1972 doctoral dissertation of Sumitra Panika, he found a reference to a letter written by Swami Nikhilananda, the founder of the Ramamkrishna Vivekananda Center in New York, the center for the study of Advaita Vedanta Hinduism. The letter discloses that Salinger studied Advaita Vendanta at the center in the early 1950s. (Eberhard Alsen. *Salinger's Glass Stories as a Composite Novel.* Troy, NY: Whitston, 1983, p. 143.)

p. 27, par. 5, In 1952, "De Daumier-Smith's Blue Period," which was, disappointingly, rejected by the *New Yorker*, was printed in London's *World Review* in May; and in 1953, "Teddy" appeared in the *New Yorker* on January 31.

p. 28, par. 1, According to Warren French, when "asked by [journalist] Betty Eppes in 1980 why he published, Salinger replied that he had not foreseen what was going to happen, and he had certainly not wanted what did happen after the publication of *The Catcher in the Rye*" (French, *Revisited,* p. 6).

p. 30, par. 2, Claire as the model for Franny was noted by several critics. *See* John Skow. "Salinger: An Introduction," reprinted in *Salinger: A Critical and Personal Portrait,* ed. Henry Anatole Grunwald. (New York: Harper and Row, 1962), p. 15; and James Lundquist. *J. D. Salinger.* (New York: Frederick Ungar, 1979), p. 30. Peggy confirmed that her mother was Franny's model. (Margaret Salinger, p. 84)

p. 32, par. 1, Peggy relates that when they became sick, the children would try to hide their illness, knowing their father would be furious with them for getting sick and furious with Claire for not feeding them the right foods. (Margaret Salinger, pp. 194–195)

p. 32, par. 2, Although she does not comment on Salinger's religious ideas, Salinger's sister agrees with Claire that Salinger destroyed his works because he did not consider them good enough. She told Peggy that her brother quit submitting his writings for publication because he wanted to be seen as "perfect. Sonny demands that, you know. He can't take any criticism." (Margaret Salinger, p. 428)

p. 33, par. 1, For further information on journalists' attempts to invade Salinger's privacy, see Ian Hamilton, pp. 167–178.

page 33, par. 3, Claire related that when she and Salinger were invited to the White House by President John F. Kennedy in spring 1963, Salinger refused to let them go; Claire sadly said that "Jerry didn't want me to feel I was worth anything, and above all, he wanted to make sure that I be prevented from having a chance to fall into the feminine vice of vanity." (quoted in Lutz, p. 34)

p. 36, par. 4, The Cornish-Windsor Bridge is the longest wooden bridge in the United States and the longest two-span bridge in the world. Built in 1866 at a cost of $9,000, it is still inscribed with its original message: "Walk your horses or pay two dollars fine."

p. 36, par. 5, Joyce Maynard said that Salinger was so totally involved in his work that his fictional Glass family "seem as real to him as the family into which he was born, and about whom he feels far greater affection" (Maynard, p. 159). In the months Joyce Maynard spent with him, Salinger never spoke of his parents or his ex-wife, and he refused to visit his sister, even when they went to Bloomingdale's where she worked, because, he explained to Joyce, "A small dose of my relatives goes a long way" (Maynard, p. 160).

p. 40, par. 1, J. D. Salinger was somehow able to win the hearts of young women, who willingly gave up their families and friends and sacrificed their own ambitions to live with him. Decades earlier, in the 1950s, one of Salinger's girlfriends, Leila Hadley, recognized that Salinger had a strong "mental power" over women. She told Ian Hamilton, "You felt he had the power to imprison someone mentally. It was as if one's mind were at risk, rather than one's virtue"(Ian Hamilton, p. 127).

Chapter 2

p. 44, par. 3, For further information on the distribution of work, *see* Foster Rhea Dulles. *Twentieth Century America.* (Boston: Houghton Mifflin), 1945, pp. 263–264.

p. 44, par. 4, Cars and related industries are discussed in Dulles, pp. 264–265.

p. 46, par. 2, For more information on the music of the 1920s, *see* Frank Freidel. *America in the Twentieth Century.* (New York: Knopf, 1960), pp. 266–272. For more information on the lifestyles of the period, see Daniel Snowman. *America Since 1920.* (New York: Harper and Row, 1968), p. 17.

p. 46, par. 3, Heroes of the 1920s are discussed in Snowman, pp. 28–29.

p. 46, par. 3, For more information on the rise of gangs, *see* Dulles, pp. 275–278.

p. 47, par. 1, For further information on prejudice during the 1920s, see the following works: Snowman, pp. 34–41; and Paul L. Murphy. "Sources and Nature of Intolerance in the 1920s," in *Reform, Crisis, and Confusion, 1900–1929,* ed. R. Jackson Wilson. (New York: Random House, 1970), pp. 182–188.

p. 47, par. 2, For more information on the predominant writers of the 1920s, see Freidel, pp. 262–266.

p. 47, par. 5, For more information on the 1920s, see the following books: Dulles, pp. 259–353; Dwight Lowell Dumond. *America in Our Time: 1896–1946.* (New York: Henry Holt, 1947), pp. 281–445; Freidel, pp. 217–275; and Snowman, pp. 11–41.

p. 49, par. 2, For further information on the 1930s, see the following books: Dulles, pp. 357–463; Dumond, pp. 469–589; Freidel, pp. 276–360; and Snowman, pp. 42–70.
p. 50, par. 2, When the atomic bomb exploded on Hiroshima, Japan, thousands of people were incinerated in a moment, and every building for miles was leveled. A mushroom-shaped cloud formed above the city, bringing black, greasy, torrential rains; then a fire wind blew into the city, burning many, while others drowned in the waves created from the wind. Daniel F. Davis and Norman Lunger. *A History of the United States Since 1945*. (New York: Scholastic, 1987), p. 18.
p. 51, par. 1, For further information on the war years, *see* the following books: Stephen E. Ambrose. *Band of Brothers: E Company 506th Regiment, 101st Airborne from Normandy to Hitler's Eagle's Nest.* (New York: Simon and Schuster, 2001); Stephen E. Ambrose. *Citizen Soldiers: The U. S. Army from the Normandy Beaches to the Bulge to the Surrender of Germany, June 7, 1944, to May 7, 1945.* (New York: Simon and Schuster, 1997); Stephen E. Ambrose. *D-Day: June 6, 1944: The Climactic Battle of World War II.* (New York: Simon and Schuster, 1994); Stephen E. Ambrose. *The Victors: Eisenhower and His Boys: The Men of World War II.* (New York: Simon and Schuster, 1998); Dulles, pp. 467–567; Dumond, pp. 590–675; Freidel, pp. 361–460; Gerden Johnson. *History of the Twelfth Infantry Regiment in World War II.* (Boston: 4th Division Association, 1947); and Snowman, pp. 103–116.
p. 51, par. 5, For further information on McCarthyism, see the following books: Davis and Norman Lunger, p. 95; and Snowman, pp. 121–124.
p. 53, par. 2, For additional information on American life in the late 1940s and 1950s, see Davis and Lunger, pp. 23–25, 67–68.
p. 53, par. 3, For further information on the late 1940s and 1950s, see the following books: Freidel, pp. 461–572; and Snowman, pp. 103–130.
p. 53, par. 5, For additional information on America's relationship with Cuba, see Davis and Lunger, pp. 149–154.
p. 55, par. 2, For additional information on the deaths of these three men, *see* Davis and Lunger, p.198.
p. 55, par. 4, For more information on the entertainment industry, *see* Davis and Lunger, pp. 128–129.
p. 55, par. 5, For further information on the 1960s, *see* Snowman, pp. 131–163.

Chapter 3

p. 62, par. 1, For further discussion on the theme of phoniness, see the following articles: Charles Kaplan. "Holden and Huck: The Odysseys of Youth," in *Critical Essays on Salinger's "The Catcher in the Rye,"* ed. Joel Salzberg. (New York: Boston: G. K. Hall, 1990), pp. 39–44; Carol Ohmann and Richard Ohmann. "Reviewers, Critics, and *The Catcher in the Rye*," *Critical Inquiry* 3, Autumn 1976, pp. 15–37; and Arthur Heiserman and James E. Miller Jr. "J. D. Salinger: Some Crazy Cliff," *Western Humanities Review* 10.2, Spring 1956, pp. 129–137.

p. 64, par. 3, For further discussion of the theme and imagery of death, see the following works: Sanford Pinsker, "The Catcher in the Rye": *Innocence Under Pressure.* (New York: Twayne, 1993), pp. 29–71; and Jane Mendelsohn. "Holden Caulfield: A Love Story," in *With Love and Squalor: 14 Writers Respond to the Work of J. D. Salinger,* ed. Kip Kotzen and Thomas Beller. (New York: Broadway Books, 2001), pp. 177–186.

p. 66, par. 2, The story of Legion is found in Matthew 8:28–34, Mark 5:1–20, and Luke 8:26–39. *New Oxford Annotated Bible.*

p. 66, par. 3, For further discussion on the motif of madness, see the following works: Pinsker. *Innocence Under Pressure,* pp. 33–49; Carl F. Strauch. "Kings in the Back Row: Meaning Through Structure, A Reading of Salinger's *The Catcher in the Rye,*" in *Studies in J. D. Salinger: Reviews, Essays, and Critiques of* "The Catcher in the Rye" *and Other Fiction,* ed. Marvin Laser and Norman Fruman. (New York: Odyssey Press, 1963), pp. 143–171.

p. 66, par. 4, For more discussion on the theme of isolation and loneliness, see the following articles: Ernest Jones. "Case History of All of Us," *Nation* 173.9, September 1, 1951, p. 176; Hans Bungert. "Salinger's *The Catcher in the Rye*: The Isolated Youth and His Struggle to Communicate," *Die Neueren Spracher*, 1960, pp. 208–217, translated from German by Wulf Griessbach, reprinted in *Studies in J. D. Salinger: Reviews, Essays, and Critiques of* The Catcher in the Rye *and Other Fiction.*, ed. Marvin Laser and Norman Fruman. (New York: Odyssey Press, 1963), pp. 177–185; Joyce Rowe. "Holden Caulfield and American Protest," in *New Essays on* "The Catcher in the Rye", ed. Jack Salzman. (Cambridge, England: Cambridge University Press, 1991), pp. 77–95.

p. 67, par. 1, For further discussion on the lack of adult guidance, see the following works: Gerald Rosen. "A Retrospective Look at *The Catcher in the Rye,*" *American Quarterly* 29.5, Winter 1977, pp. 547–562; and

Robert Miltner. "Mentor Mori: or, Sibling Society and the *Catcher* in the Bly," in "The Catcher in the Rye": *New Essays*, ed. J. P. Steed. (New York: Peter Lang, 2002), pp. 33–52.

p. 68, par. 2. Donald P. Costello notes that in the 1950s "reviewers in the *Chicago Sun Tribune*, the *London Times Literary Supplement*, the *New Republic*, the *New York Herald Tribune Book Review*, the *New York Times*, the *New Yorker*, and *Saturday Review of Literature* all specifically mentioned the authenticity of the book's language" (92). He states that only two religious magazines, *Catholic World* and the *Christian Science Monitor*, did not find the language authentic, for they "refused to believe that the 'obscenity' was realistic" (93). (Donald P. Costello. "The Language of "*The Catcher in the Rye*," in *Studies in J. D. Salinger: Reviews, Essays, and Critiques of* The Catcher in the Rye *and Other Fiction*, ed. Laser and Fruman. pp. 92–93.)

p. 69, par. 1, For more information about Salinger's use of language, see the following works: Costello, pp. 92–104; and Clifford Mills. "A Critical Perspective on the Writing of J. D. Salinger, "in *Bloom's BioCritiques: J. D. Salinger*, ed. Harold Bloom. (Philadelphia: Chelsea House, 2002), p. 46.

p. 70, par. 2, For further information on the character of Holden, see the following works: Mark Silverberg. "'You Must Change Your Life': Formative Responses to *The Catcher in the Rye*," in *New Essays*, ed. J. P. Steed. pp. 7–32; Pinsker, *Innocence Under Pressure*, pp. 89–98; and Rowe, 79–92. For a psychological analysis of Holden, see James Bryan. "The Psychological Structure of *The Catcher in the* Rye," *PMLA* 89.5, 1974, pp. 1065–1074. For an analysis of the psychological interpretations of Holden, see Peter Shaw. "Love and Death in *The Catcher in the Rye*," in *New Essays*, ed. Jack Salzman, pp. 97–114.

p. 72, par. 1, For further information on the structure of the novel, see the following works: Clinton W. Trowbridge. "The Symbolic Structure of *The Catcher in the Rye*," in *Modern Critical Interpretations: J. D. Salinger's* "The Catcher in the Rye", ed. Harold Bloom. (Philadelphia: Chelsea House, 2000), pp. 21–30; Brian Way. "A Tight Three-Movement Structure," from " 'Franny and Zooey' and J. D. Salinger," by Brian Way, *New Left Review*, May–June 1962, pp. 72–82, reprinted in *Studies in J. D. Salinger: Reviews, Essays, and Critiques of* The Catcher in the Rye *and Other Fiction*, ed. Marvin Laser and Norman Fruman. (New York: Odyssey Press, 1963), pp. 190–201; and Clifford Mills. "A Critical

Perspective on the Writing of J. D. Salinger, "in *Bloom's BioCritiques: J. D. Salinger,* ed. Harold Bloom. (Philadelphia: Chelsea House, 2002).

page 73, par. 2, For further information on prep schools, see Christopher Brookeman. "Pencey Preppy: Cultural Modes in *The Catcher in the Rye,*" in *New Essays*, ed. Jack Salzman, pp. 57–76.

p. 76, par. 2, For further information on the museum displays, see Michael Cowan. "Holden's Museum Pieces: Narrator and Nominal Audience in *The Catcher in the Rye,*" in *New Essays*, pp. 35–55.

p. 80, par. 2, In 1991, Grayslake, Illinois challengers objected to its profanity. (Karolides, Bald, and Sova, 367). The following year, four challenges to the novel appeared: parents in Sidell, Illinois, were bothered by "profanities and the depiction of premarital sex, alcohol abuse, and prostitution"; people in Waterloo, Iowa, and Duval County, Florida, found "the 'lurid passages about sex' and profanity" offensive; and a parent at Carlisle, Pennsylvania, was disturbed by the "immoral" book that used profanity (Karolides, Bald, and Sova, 367–368). In 1993, parents of the Corona–Norco School District in California were offended by the book because it "centered around negative activity" (Karolides, Bald, and Sova, 367–368). The following year it was challenged in New Richmond, Wisconsin, and Goffstown, New Hampshire, because of its use of "vulgar words" and the protagonist's "sexual exploits" (Karolides, Bald, and Sova, 367–368).

Chapter 4

p. 84, par. 1, James E. Miller Jr. explains that the primary theme of all the stories is "alienation," which is sometimes the fault of society, as in racial prejudice or war; sometimes the "failure of personal relationships"; and sometimes the fault of a sensitive individual. (James E. Miller Jr. *J. D. Salinger.* University of Minnesota Pamphlet on American Writers, no. 51. Minneapolis: University of Minnesota Press, 1965, p. 20.) For more information on the relationships of the stories, see Warren French. *J. D. Salinger, Revisited.* (Boston: Twayne, 1988), p. 63; and John Wenke. *J. D. Salinger: A Study of the Short Fiction.* (Boston: Twayne, 1991), p. 34.

p. 84, par. 2, For more information on Zen *koans,* see Bernice Goldstein and Sanford Goldstein. "Zen and *Nine Stories,*" in *Modern Critical Views: J. D. Salinger,* ed. Harold Bloom. (New York: Chelsea House, 1987), p. 82; James Lundquist. *J. D. Salinger.* (New York: Frederick Ungar,

1979), pp. 74–78; Dominic Smith. "Salinger's *Nine Stories:* Fifty Years Later," *Antioch Review* 61.4, Fall 2003, p. 641; Clifford Mills, "A Critical Perspective on the Writings of J. D. Salinger," in *Bloom's BioCritiques: J. D. Salinger,* ed. Harold Bloom. (Philadelphia: Chelsea House, 2002), p. 50; Gerald Rosen. "A Retrospective Look at *The Catcher in the Rye,*" *American Quarterly* 29.5, Winter 1977, pp. 547–562.

p. 85, par. 2, James Lundquist explains that Seymour is on a Zen spiritual journey of self-discovery in which he attempts to "see more." These are the words Sybil uses in the story when she asks, "Did you see more glass?" (10–11) Seymour finds the physical world revolting and decides to commit suicide. Lundquist explains that Seymour's exchanges with Sybil support his view. For instance, Seymour invites Sybil to see herself in a new way, wearing a blue (associated with spirituality) bathing suit instead of the yellow (associated with the physical) one she has on. His suicide is his way of evading the phony world of his wife (Lundquist, pp. 82–87).

p. 87, par. 3, For a detailed analysis of "The Laughing Man," see Richard Allan Davison. "Salinger Criticism and 'The Laughing Man': A Case of Arrested Development," *Studies in Short Fiction* 18.1, Winter 1981, pp. 1–15.

p. 90, par. 2, David D. Galloway explains that De Daumier is much like Holden Caulfield, a young man hypersensitive to the phoniness of the world because of an absence of love. (David D. Galloway. "The Love Ethic," in *Modern Critical Views: J. D. Salinger,* ed. Harold Bloom. (New York: Chelsea House, 1987), p. 34.

p. 91, par. 3, Anthony Kaufman tries to persuade readers that "Teddy" is a successful story because Teddy is not a "detached mystical prodigy, but . . . an unloved, frightened 10-year-old" (129). But this reading dismisses Salinger's portrayal of Teddy as a mystical seer. For a complete analysis of this point of view, see Anthony Kaufman. "'Along this road goes no one': Salinger's 'Teddy' and the Failure of Love," *Studies in Short Fiction* 35.2, Spring 1998, pp. 129–140.

p. 95, par. 2. Salinger's religious ideas are examined by Eberhard Alsen in *Salinger's Glass Stories as a Composite Novel.* He explains that critics generally see "Zen Buddhism as the major component of the Glass philosophy." However, Buddy, in "Seymour—An Introduction," explains that their religious ideas have "roots in Eastern philosophy" and were planted "in the New and Old Testaments, Advaita Vendata, and classical Taoism." (208) According to Alsen, Zen Buddhism, which originated in India, teaches believers to search for God, "an impersonal essence inherent in all things . . . [which] cannot be known by the mind, only by the heart" (128) through meditation and intuitive perception. Taoism is similar. It promotes "the conception of an abstract Godhead inherent in all things, the emphasis on intuitive perception of this ultimate essence, and the insistence on detachment . . . to achieve harmony with the natural order of things." (Alsen, 138) Vedanta Hinduism teaches that "Brahman—the absolute existence, knowledge, and bliss—is real. The universe is not real. Brahman and Atman (man's inner self) are One." (Shankaracharya quoted in Alsen, 144) It emphasizes knowledge as the way to enlightenment and teaches the need for meditation exercises (Alsen, 145). Christian ideas are mixed with Jewish and Eastern thought. For Salinger, Christ is not part of the triune God but is merely human, an enlightened man. (Alsen, 141–142) For more information on Salinger's religious ideas, see Eberhard Alsen. *Salinger's Glass Stories as a Composite Novel.* (Troy, NY: Whitston, 1983), pp. 123–164.

p. 97, par. 2. For further reactions of contemporary young authors to Salinger's works, see the essays in eds., Kip Kotzen and Thomas Beller. *With Love and Squalor: 14 Writers Respond to the Work of J. D. Salinger.* (New York: Broadway Books, 2001).

p. 99, par. 1, Most critics do not examine the structure of the story and therefore assume that Seymour is the protagonist. See William Wiegand. "J. D. Salinger: Seventy-Eight Bananas," in *Salinger: A Critical and Personal Portrait,* ed. Henry Anatole Grunwald. (New York: Harper and Row, 1962), pp. 123–136; and Ihab Hassan. *Radical Innocence: Studies in the Contemporary American Novel.* (Princeton, NJ: Princeton University Press, 1961), pp. 279–281.

p. 99, par. 3, For further explanation on the structure of "Raise High the Roof Beam, Carpenters" and Buddy as protagonist, see Alsen, *Glass Stories,* pp. 33–47.

p. 100, par. 1, For further information on the structure of "Seymour: An Introduction" and the character of Seymour, see Alsen, *Glass Stories,* pp. 63–77; and Warren French, *J. D. Salinger.* (New York: Twayne, 1963), pp. 155–160; and French. *Revisited*, pp. 107–109.

Chapter 5

p. 105, par. 1, One critic who believes that Salinger's work is a "minor classic" is George Steiner. In 1959, he argued that Salinger is a good minor writer with only one novel. Although Salinger is "a most skillful and original writer" who is "worth discussing and praising," he is not one of "the master poets of the world." His stories are not "the house of Atreus reborn." (George Steiner. "The Salinger Industry," in *Salinger: A Critical and Personal Portrait,* ed. Henry Anatole Grunwald. New York: Harper and Row, 1962, p. 85).

p. 106, par. 1, The collections include the following: eds. William F. Belcher and James W. Lee, *Salinger and the Critics.* (Belmont, CA: Wadsworth, 1962); Henry Anatole Grunwald, ed. *Salinger: A Critical and Personal Portrait.* (New York: Harper and Row, 1962); eds., Marvin Laser and Norman Fruman, *Studies in J. D. Salinger; Reviews, Essays, and Critiques of* The Catcher in the Rye *and Other Fiction.* (New York: Odyssey Press, 1963); ed. Malcolm M. Marsden, *If You Really Want to Know: A Catcher Casebook.* (Chicago: Scott, Foresman, 1963); and eds. Harold P. Simonson and Philip E. Hager, *Salinger's "Catcher in the Rye": Clamor vs. Criticism.* (Boston: Heath, 1963). Special Salinger issues were brought out by *Wisconsin Studies in Contemporary Literature* 4.1, Winter 1963; and *Modern Fiction Studies* 12.3, Autumn 1966.

p. 106, par. 2. Major works published in the 1980s were Eberhard Alsen's thorough analysis of the Glass family stories, *Salinger's Glass Stories as a Composite Novel,* Warren French's *J. D. Salinger, Revisited,* Jack R. Sublette's *J. D. Salinger: An Annotated Bibliography, 1938–1981,* and Ian Hamilton's *In Search of J. D. Salinger.* In the 1990s only two important additions to Salinger scholarship appeared: Sanford Pinsker's "The Catcher in the Rye": *Innocence Under Pressure* (1993) and Paul Alexander's *Salinger: A Biography* (1999).

p. 107, par. 1, The censorship has not been confined to secondary schools. In 1961, the attorney father of a University of Texas student was so upset when his daughter was assigned Salinger's novel that he "threatened to remove the girl from the University," arguing that "Salinger used language no sane person would use and accus[ing] the university of 'corrupting the moral fibers [sic] of our youth'" (Willie Morris. "Houston's Superpatriots," *Harper's* Magazine).

p. 108, par. 1, For a deliberation of the role Salinger's *The Catcher in the Rye* played in Mark Chapman's murder of John Lennon, see Daniel M. Stashower. "On First Looking into Chapman's Holden: Speculations on a Murder," *American Scholar* 52, 1983, pp. 373–377.

p. 109, par. 3, For an analysis of the Jerry Salinger character in W. P. Kinsella's book, see Dennis Cutchins. "*Catcher* in the Corn: J. D. Salinger and *Shoeless Joe,*" in "The Catcher in the Rye": *New Essays,* ed. J. P. Steed, pp. 53–77.

p. 109, par. 3, For an analysis of the changes made to Jerry Salinger's character in the *Field of Dreams* screenplay, see Joseph S. Walker. "The Catcher Takes the Field: Holden, Hollywood, and the Making of a Mann," in *New Essays*, ed. J. P. Steed, pp. 79–99.

p. 110, par. 1, The following literary works include references to Salinger or his novel: John Fowles. *The Collector.* (Boston: Little, Brown, 1963); W. P. Kinsella. *Shoeless Joe.* (New York: Ballantine Books, 1982); John Guare. *Six Degrees of Separation.* (New York: Random House, 1990); and Eve Horowitz. *Plain Jane.* (New York: Random House, 1992). Three works were made into Hollywood films: (1). *The Collector.* Dir. William Wyler. Columbia Pictures. 1965; (2). *Field of Dreams.* Based on *Shoeless Joe.* Dir. Phil Alden Robinson. Universal Pictures. 1989; (3). *Six Degrees of Separation.* Dir. Fred Schepisi. MGM/United Artists Studios. 1993. In addition, Salinger's book is mentioned in this film: *Guilty By Suspicion.* Dir. Irwin Winkler. Warner Brothers. 1990.

Further Reading

1. Books by J. D. Salinger

Salinger, J. D. *The Catcher in the Rye.* Boston: Little, Brown, 1951.

———. *The Complete Uncollected Short Stories of J. D. Salinger.* 2 vols. Berkeley, CA: private printing, 1974.

———. *Franny and Zooey.* Boston: Little, Brown, 1961.

———. *Nine Stories.* Boston: Little, Brown, 1953.

———. *Raise High the Roof Beam, Carpenters and Seymour: An Introduction.* Boston: Little, Brown, 1963.

2. Books about J. D. Salinger's Life and Works

Alexander, Paul. *Salinger: A Biography.* Los Angeles: Renaissance Books, 1999.

Hamilton, Ian. *In Search of J. D. Salinger: A Biography.* New York: Vintage Books, 1989.

Salinger, Margaret Ann. *Dream Catcher: A Memoir.* New York: Washington Square Press, 2000.

3. Critical Collections

Bloom, Harold, ed. *Bloom's BioCritiques: J. D. Salinger.* Philadelphia: Chelsea House, 2002.

———. *Modern Critical Interpretations: J. D. Salinger's* The Catcher in the Rye. Philadelphia: Chelsea House, 2000.

———. *Modern Critical Views: J. D. Salinger.* New York: Chelsea House, 1987.

Kotzen, Kip and Thomas Beller, eds. *With Love and Squalor: 14 Writers Respond to the Work of J. D. Salinger.* New York: Broadway Books, 2001.

Salzberg, Joel, ed. *Critical Essays on Salinger's* The Catcher in the Rye. Boston: G. K. Hall, 1990.

Salzman, Jack, ed. *New Essays on* The Catcher in the Rye. Cambridge: Cambridge University Press, 1991.

Steed, J. P., ed. "The Catcher in the Rye": *New Essays*. New York: Peter Lang, 2002.

4. Books about J. D. Salinger's Times

Ambrose, Stephen E. *Band of Brothers: E Company, 506th Regiment, 101st Airborne from Normandy to Hitler's Eagle's Nest*. New York: Simon and Schuster, 2001.

Davis, Daniel F., and Norman Lunger. *A History of the United States Since 1945*. New York: Scholastic, 1987.

Web Sites

http://www.deadcaulfields.com
Contains a biography, pictures, and discussions of *Catcher in the Rye* and *Nine Stories*.

http://www.levity.com/corduroy/salinger.htm
Includes a brief biography, excerpts from the works, literary criticism and analysis, a plot synopsis of *Catcher in the Rye*, electronic texts, and links.

http://www.morrill.org/books/salbio.shtml
Consists of a biography written in question-and-answer format.

http://www.salinger.org
Includes information on Salinger's stories and characters, as well as readers' opinions and miscellaneous information.

Bibliography

Works by J. D. Salinger

Salinger, J. D. "Blue Melody." *Cosmopolitan* 125 (September 1948), pp. 50–51, 112–119.

———. "Both Parties Concerned." *Saturday Evening Post* 216 (February 26, 1944), pp. 14, 47–48.

———. "A Boy in France." *Saturday Evening Post* 217 (March 31, 1945), pp. 21, 92.

———. *The Catcher in the Rye*. Boston: Little, Brown, 1951.

———. *The Complete Uncollected Short Stories of J. D. Salinger*. 2 vols. Berkeley: private printing, 1974.

———. "De Daumier-Smith's Blue Period." *World Review* (London) 39 (May 1952), pp. 33–48.

———. "Down at the Dinghy." *Harper's* magazine 198 (April 1949), pp. 87–91.

———. "Elaine." *Story* 26 (March–April 1945), pp. 38–47.

———. "Epilogue: A Salute to Whit Burnett, 1899–1972." In Hallie and Whit Burnett, *Fiction Writer's Handbook*. 187–188. New York: Harper and Row, 1975.

———. "For Esmé—with Love and Squalor." *The New Yorker* 26 (April 8, 1950), pp. 28–36.

———. "Franny." *New Yorker* 30 (January 29, 1955), pp. 24–32, 35–43.

———. *Franny and Zooey*. Boston: Little, Brown, 1961.

———. "A Girl I Knew." *Good Housekeeping* 126 (February 1948), pp. 37, 186, 188, 191–196.

———. "Go See Eddie." *University of Kansas City Review* 7 (December 1940), pp. 121–124.

———. "The Hang of It." *Collier's* 108 (July 12, 1941), p. 22.

———. "Hapworth 16, 1924." *The New Yorker* 41 (June 19, 1965), pp. 32–113.

———. "The Heart of a Broken Story." *Esquire* 16 (September 1941), pp. 32, 131–133.

———. "I'm Crazy." *Collier's* 116 (December 22, 1945), pp. 36, 48, 51.

———. “The Inverted Forest.” *Cosmopolitan* 113 (December 1947), pp. 73–80, 85–86, 88, 90, 92, 95–96, 98, 100, 102, 107, 109.

———. “Just Before the War with the Eskimos.” *The New Yorker* 24 (June 5,1948), pp. 37–40, 42, 44, 46.

———. “Last Day of the Last Furlough.” *Saturday Evening Post* 217 (July 15, 1944), pp. 26–27, 61–62, 64.

———. “The Laughing Man.” *The New Yorker* 25 (March 19, 1949), pp. 27–32.

———. “The Long Debut of Lois Taggett.” *Story* 21 (September–October 1942), pp. 28–34.

———. “Man-Forsaken Man.” *New York Post Magazine,* December 9, 1955, 49.

———. *Nine Stories.* Boston: Little, Brown, 1953.

———. “Once a Week Won’t Kill You.” *Story* 25 (November–December 1944), pp. 23–27.

———. “A Perfect Day for Bananafish.” *The New Yorker* 23 (January 31, 1948), pp. 21–25.

———. “Personal Notes on an Infantryman.” *Collier’s* 110 (December 12, 1942), p. 96.

———. “Pretty Mouth and Green My Eyes.” *The New Yorker* 27 (July 14, 1951), pp. 20–24.

———. “Raise High the Roof Beam, Carpenters.” *The New Yorker* 31 (November 19, 1955), pp. 51–58, 60–116.

———. *Raise High the Roof Beam, Carpenters and Seymour: An Introduction.* Boston: Little, Brown, 1963.

———. “Seymour: An Introduction.” *The New Yorker* 35 (June 6, 1959), pp. 42–52, 54–111.

———. “Slight Rebellion Off Madison.” *The New Yorker* 22 (December 21, 1946), pp. 76–79.

———. “Soft-Boiled Sergeant.” *Saturday Evening Post* 216 (April 15, 1944), pp. 18, 82, 84–85.

———. “The Stranger.” *Collier’s* 116 (December 1, 1945), pp. 18, 77.

———. “Teddy.” *The New Yorker* 28 (31 January 1953), pp. 26–36, 38.

———. “This Sandwich Has No Mayonnaise.” *Esquire* 24 (October 1945), pp. 54–56, 147–149.

———. “Uncle Wiggily in Connecticut.” *The New Yorker* 24 (March 20, 1948), pp. 30–36.

———. "The Varioni Brothers." *Saturday Evening Post* 216 (July 17, 1943), pp. 12–13, 76–77.

———. "The Young Folks." *Story* 16 (March–April 1940), pp. 26–30.

———. "A Young Girl in 1941 with No Waist at All." *Mademoiselle* 25 (May 1947), pp. 222–223, 292–302.

———. "Zooey." *The New Yorker* 33 (4 May 1957), pp. 32–42, 44–139.

Other Works

Alexander, Paul. *Salinger: A Biography.* Los Angeles: Renaissance Books, 1999.

Alsen, Eberhard. "'Raise High the Roofbeam, [sic] Carpenters' and the Amateur Reader." *Studies in Short Fiction* 17.1 (Winter 1980), pp. 39–47.

———. *Salinger's Glass Stories as a Composite Novel.* Troy, NY: Whitston, 1983.

Ambrose, Stephen E. *Band of Brothers: E Company, 506th Regiment, 101st Airborne from Normandy to Hitler's Eagle's Nest.* New York: Simon and Schuster, 2001.

———. *Citizen Soldiers: The U. S. Army from the Normandy Beaches to the Bulge to the Surrender of Germany, June 7, 1944, to May 7, 1945.* New York: Simon and Schuster, 1997.

———. *D-Day, June 6, 1944: The Climactic Battle of World War II.* New York: Simon and Schuster, 1994.

———. *The Victors: Eisenhower and His Boys: The Men of World War II.* New York: Simon and Schuster, 1998.

Baker, Carlos. *Ernest Hemingway: A Life Story*. New York: Scribner's, 1969.

Baskett, Sam S. "The Splendid/Squalid World of J. D. Salinger." In "Special Number: Salinger." *Wisconsin Studies in Contemporary Literature* 4.1 (Winter 1963), pp. 48–61.

Baumbach, Jonathan. "The Saint as a Young Man: A Reappraisal of *The Catcher in the Rye.*" in Joel Salzberg, ed. *Critical Essays*, 55–64.

Belcher, William F. and James W. Lee, eds. *Salinger and the Critics.* Belmont, CA: Wadsworth, 1962.

Bloom, Harold, ed. *Bloom's BioCritiques: J. D. Salinger.* Philadelphia: Chelsea House, 2002.

———. "Introduction." In Bloom, ed. *Bloom's BioCritiques.*

———. *Modern Critical Interpretations: J. D. Salinger's* "The Catcher in the Rye." Philadelphia: Chelsea House, 2000.
———. *Modern Critical Views: J. D. Salinger.* New York: Chelsea House, 1987.
Breit, Harvey. "Reader's Choice." *Atlantic* 188 (August 1951), p. 82.
Brookeman, Christopher. "Pencey Preppy: Cultural Modes in *The Catcher in the Rye.*" In Jack Salzman, ed. *New Essays.*
Bryan, James. "The Psychological Structure of *The Catcher in the* Rye." *PMLA* 89.5 (1974), pp. 1065–1074.
Bungert, Hans. "Salinger's *The Catcher in the Rye*: The Isolated Youth and His Struggle to Communicate." *Die Neueren Sprachen* (1960), pp. 208–217. Translated by Wulf Griessbach.
Catholic World. Review of *The Catcher in the Rye.*" by J. D. Salinger. 174.1040 (November 1951), p. 154. Reprinted in Joel Salzberg, ed. *Critical Essays on Salinger's* The Catcher in the Rye. 25–28. Boston: G. K. Hall, 1990.
The Collector. Based on *The Collector* by John Fowles. Dir. by William Wyler. Columbia Pictures. 1965.
Corbett, Edward P. J. "Raise High the Barriers, Censors." In Laser and Fruman, eds. *Studies in J. D. Salinger*. 134–141.
Costello, Donald P. "The Language of *The Catcher in the Rye.*" In Laser and Fruman, eds. *Studies in J. D. Salinger*. 92–104.
Cowan, Michael. "Holden's Museum Pieces: Narrator and Nominal Audience in *The Catcher in the Rye.*" In Salzman, ed. *New Essays.* 35–55.
Cutchins, Dennis. "*Catcher* in the Corn: J. D. Salinger and *Shoeless Joe.*" In Steed, ed. *New Essays. 53–77.*
D'Ambrosio, Charles. "Salinger and Sobs." In Kotzen and Beller, eds. *With Love and Squalor.* 27–54.
Davis, Daniel F. and Norman Lunger. *A History of the United States Since 1945.* New York: Scholastic, 1987.
Davison, Richard Allan. "Salinger Criticism and 'The Laughing Man': A Case of Arrested Development." *Studies in Short Fiction* 18.1 (Winter 1981), pp. 1–15.
DeLillo, Don. *Mao II.* New York: Viking Penguin, 1991.
Didion, Joan. "Finally (Fashionably) Spurious." In Laser and Fruman, eds. *Studies in J. D. Salinger.* 232–234.

Dulles, Foster Rhea. *Twentieth Century America.* Boston: Houghton Mifflin, 1945.
Dumond, Dwight Lowell. *America in Our Time: 1896–1946.* New York: Henry Holt and Company, 1947.
Engle, Paul. "Honest Tale of Distraught Adolescent." In Marsden, ed. *A Catcher Casebook.* 4–5. Chicago: Scott, Foresman, 1963.
Evertson, Matt. "Love, Loss, and Growing Up in J. D. Salinger and Cormac McCarthy." In Steed, ed. *New Essays.* 101–141.
Fiedler, Leslie. "Up from Adolescence." In Laser and Fruman, eds. *Studies in J. D. Salinger.* 235–240.
Field of Dreams. Dir. by Phil Alden Robinson. Based on *Shoeless Joe* by W. P. Kinsella.Universal Pictures. 1989.
Fowles, John. *The Collector.* Boston: Little, Brown, 1963.
Freidel, Frank. *America in the Twentieth Century.* New York: Knopf, 1960.
French, Warren. *J. D. Salinger.* New York: Twayne, 1963.
———. *J. D. Salinger, Revisited.* Boston: Twayne, 1988.
Galloway, David D. "The Love Ethic." Bloom, ed. *Modern Critical Views.* 29–51. New York: Chelsea House, 1987.
Geismar, Maxwell. "J. D. Salinger: The Wise Child and the *New Yorker* School of Fiction." *American Moderns: From Rebellion to Conformity.* New York: Hill and Wang, 1958, 195–209.
Goldstein, Bernice and Sanford Goldstein. "Zen and *Nine Stories.*" In Bloom, ed. *Modern Critical Views.* 81–93.
Goodman, Anne L. "Mad Abut Children." In Salzberg, ed. *Critical Essays.* 23–24.
Green, Jonathon. *The Encyclopedia of Censorship.* New York: Facts on File, 1990.
Grunwald, Henry Anatole. "The Invisible Man: A Biographical Collage." In Grunwald, ed. *Salinger.*
———, ed. *Salinger: A Critical and Personal Portrait.* New York: Harper and Row, 1962.
Guare, John. *Six Degrees of Separation.* New York: Random House, 1990.
Guilty By Suspicion. Dir. by Irwin Winkler. Warner Brothers. 1990.
Gutwillig, Robert. "Everybody's Caught *The Catcher in the Rye.*" In Laser and Fruman, eds. *Studies in J. D. Salinger.* 1–5.
Gwynn, Frederick L. and Joseph L. Blotner. *The Fiction of J. D. Salinger.*

Pittsburgh: University of Pittsburgh Press, 1958.

Haight, Anne Lyon. *Banned Books: 387 B.C. to 1978 A.D.* 4th ed. Updated and enlarged by Chandler B. Grannis. New York: R. R. Bowker, 1978.

Hamilton, Ian. *In Search of J. D. Salinger: A Biography.* New York: Vintage Books, 1989.

Hamilton, Kenneth. *J. D. Salinger: A Critical Essay*. Grand Rapids, MI: Eerdmans, 1967.

Hassan, Ihab. *Radical Innocence: Studies in the Contemporary American Novel.* Princeton, NJ: Princeton University Press, 1961, pp. 260–289.

Heiserman, Arthur and James E. Miller Jr. "J. D. Salinger: Some Crazy Cliff." *Western Humanities Review* 10.2 (Spring 1956), 32–39.

Heman, Aleksander. "The Importance of Wax and Olives." In Kotzen and Beller, eds. *With Love and Squalor.* 62–77.

Hicks, Granville. "J. D. Salinger: Search for Wisdom." In Laser and Fruman, eds. *Studies in J. D. Salinger*. 88–91.

Horowitz, Eve. *Plain Jane.* New York: Random House, 1992.

"J. D. Salinger 'Special Number.'" *Modern Fiction Studies* 12.3 (Autumn 1966), 297–390.

Johnson, Gerden. *History of the Twelfth Infantry Regiment in World War II.* Boston: 4th Division Association, 1947.

Jones, Ernest. "Case History of All of Us." *Nation* 173.9 (September 1, 1951), p. 176.

Kaplan, Charles. "Holden and Huck: The Odysseys of Youth." In Salzberg, ed. *Critical Essays*. 39–44.

Karolides, Nicholas J., Margaret Bald, and Dawn B. Sova. *100 Banned Books: Censorship Histories of World Literature.* New York: Checkmark Books, 1999.

Kaufman, Anthony. "'Along this road goes no one': Salinger's 'Teddy' and the Failure of Love." *Studies in Short Fiction* 35.2 (Spring 1998), pp. 129–140.

Kazin, Alfred. "J. D. Salinger: 'Everybody's Favorite.'" In Bloom, ed. *Bloom's BioCritiques*. 67–75.

Kinsella, W. P. *Shoeless Joe.* New York: Ballantine Books, 1982.

Kotzen, Kip and Thomas Beller, eds. *With Love and Squalor: 14 Writers Respond to the Work of J. D. Salinger.* New York: Broadway Books, 2001.

Laser, Marvin and Norman Fruman, eds. "Not Suitable for Temple City." *Studies in J. D. Salinger*. 124–129.

———. "Salinger: The Early Reviews." In Laser and Fruman, eds. *Studies in J. D. Salinger*. 6–22.

———, eds. *Studies in J. D. Salinger: Reviews, Essays, and Critiques of* "The Catcher in the Rye" *and Other Fiction*. New York: Odyssey Press, 1963.

Longstreth, T. Morris. "Review of *The Catcher in the Rye.*" In Joel Salzberg, ed. *Critical Essays*. 30–31.

Lundquist, James. *J. D. Salinger.* New York: Frederick Ungar, 1979.

Lutz, Norma Jean. "Biography of J. D. Salinger." In Bloom, ed. *Bloom's BioCritiques*. 3–44.

Marcus, Jacob R. *Studies in American Jewish History.* Cincinnati: Hebrew Union College Press, 1969.

Marple, Anne. "Salinger's Oasis of Innocence." In Laser and Fruman, eds. *Studies in J. D. Salinger*. 241–244.

Marsden, Malcolm M., ed. *If You Really Want to Know: A Catcher Casebook*. Chicago: Scott, Foresman, 1963.

Maynard, Joyce. *At Home in the World: A Memoir.* New York: Picador, 1998.

McCarthy, Cormac. *All the Pretty Horses*. New York: First Vintage International Edition, 1993.

McCarthy, Mary. "J. D. Salinger's Closed Circuit." In Laser and Fruman, eds. *Studies in J. D. Salinger.* 245–250.

Mendelsohn, Jane. "Holden Caulfield: A Love Story." In Kotzen and Beller, eds. *With Love and Squalor.* 177–186.

Miller, James E. Jr. *J. D. Salinger*. University of Minnesota Pamphlets on American Writers, no. 51. Minneapolis: University of Minnesota Press, 1965.

Mills, Clifford. "A Critical Perspective on the Writings of J. D. Salinger." In Bloom, ed. *Bloom's BioCritiques*. 45–66.

Miltner, Robert. "Mentor Mori: or, Sibling Society and the *Catcher* in the Bly." In Steed, ed. *New Essays*. 33–52.

Mizener, Arthur. "The Love Song of J. D. Salinger." In Laser and Fruman, eds. *Studies in J. D. Salinger*. 202–215.

Morris, Willie. "Houston's Superpatriots." *Harper's* magazine (October 1961), p. 50.

Murphy, Paul L. "Sources and Nature of Intolerance in the 1920s." In R. Jackson Wilson, ed. *Reform, Crisis, and Confusion, 1900–1929*. 179–196. New York: Random House, 1970.

New Oxford Annotated Bible with the Apocryphal/Deuterocanonical

Books. Ed. Bruce M. Metzger and Roland E. Murphy. New Revised Standard Version. New York: Oxford University Press, 1994.

Ohmann, Carol and Richard Ohmann. "Reviewers, Critics, and *The Catcher in the Rye*." *Critical Inquiry* 3 (Autumn 1976), pp. 15–37.

Peterson, Virgilia. "Three Days in the Bewildering World of an Adolescent." In Malcolm M. Marsden, ed. *A Catcher Casebook*. 3–4.

Pinsker, Sanford. "*The Catcher in the Rye* and All: Is the Age of the Formative Book Over?" *Georgia Review* 40 (1986), pp. 953–967.

———. "The Catcher in the Rye"*: Innocence Under Pressure*. New York: Twayne, 1993.

Poster, William. "Tomorrow's Child." In Salzberg, ed. *Critical Essays*. 25–28.

Rosen, Gerald. "A Retrospective Look at *The Catcher in the Rye*." *American Quarterly* 29.5 (Winter 1977), pp. 547–562.

Rosenfeld, Lucinda. "The Trouble with Franny." In Kotzen and Beller, eds. *With Love and Squalor*. 78–87.

Rowe, Joyce. "Holden Caulfield and American Protest." In Salzman, ed. *New Essays*. 77–95.

Salinger, Margaret Ann. *Dream Catcher: A Memoir*. New York: Washington Square Press, 2000.

Salzberg, Joel, ed. *Critical Essays on Salinger's* "The Catcher in the Rye." Boston: G. K. Hall, 1990.

———. "Introduction." In Salzberg, ed. *Critical Essays*. 1–22.

Salzman, Jack. "Introduction." In Jack Salzman, ed. *New Essays on* The Catcher in the Rye. 1–22. Cambridge: Cambridge University Press, 1991.

———. *New Essays on* "The Catcher in the Rye." Cambridge: Cambridge University Press, 1991.

Samuels, David. "Marginal Notes on *Franny and Zooey*." *American Scholar* 68.3 (Summer 1999), pp. 128–133.

Schriber, Mary Suzanne. "Holden Caulfield, C'est Moi." In Salzberg, ed. *Critical Essays*. 226–238. Boston.

Seelye, John. "Holden in the Museum." In Salzman, ed. *New Essays*. 22–33.

Shaw, Peter. "Love and Death in *The Catcher in the Rye*." In Salzman, ed. *New Essays*. 97–114.

Silverberg, Mark. "'You Must Change Your Life': Formative Responses to *The Catcher in the Rye*." In Steed, ed. *New Essays*. 7–32.

Simonson, Harold P. and Philip E. Hager, eds. *Salinger's "Catcher in the*

Rye": Clamor vs. Criticism. Boston: Heath, 1963.

Six Degrees of Separation. Dir. by Fred Schepisi. Based on *Six Degrees of Separation* by John Guare. MGM/United Artists Studios. 1993.

Skow, John. "Salinger: An Introduction." In Grunwald, ed. *Salinger.* 3–18.

Smith, Dominic. "Salinger's *Nine Stories:* Fifty Years Later." *Antioch Review* 61.4 (Fall 2003), pp. 639–649.

Smith, Harrison. "Manhattan Ulysses, Junior." In Salzberg, ed. *Critical Essays*. 28–30.

Snowman, Daniel. *America Since 1920*. New York: Harper and Row, 1968.

Sohn, Amy. "Franny and Amy." In Kotzen and Beller, eds. *With Love and Squalor.* 88–103.

"Special Number: Salinger." *Wisconsin Studies in Contemporary Literature* 4.1 (Winter 1963), 1–160.

Stashower, Daniel M. "On First Looking into Chapman's Holden: Speculations on a Murder." *American Scholar* 52 (1983), pp. 373–377.

Steed, J. P., ed. "The Catcher in the Rye": *New Essays*. New York: Peter Lang, 2002.

———. "Introduction: *The Catcher in the Rye* at Fifty, 1951–2001." In J. P. Steed, ed. The Catcher in the Rye: *New Essays*. 1–5. New York: Peter Lang, 2002.

Steiner, George. "The Salinger Industry." In Grunwald, ed. *Salinger.* 82–85.

Stern, James. "Aw, the World's a Crumby Place." In Marsden, ed. *A Catcher Casebook*. 2–3.

Strauch, Carl F. "Kings in the Back Row: Meaning Through Structure, A Reading of Salinger's *The Catcher in the Rye.*" In Laser and Fruman, eds. *Studies in J. D. Salinger*. 143–171. New York: Odyssey Press, 1963.

Sublette, Jack R. *J. D. Salinger: An Annotated Bibliography, 1938–1981*. New York: Garland, 1984.

Swados, Harvey. "Must Writers be Characters?" In Laser and Fruman, eds. *Studies in J. D. Salinger.* 119–121.

Trowbridge, Clinton W. In Harold Bloom, ed. *Modern Critical Interpretations*. 21–30.

Updike, John. In Grunwald, ed. *Salinger.* 53–56. New York: Harper and Row, 1962.

Walker, Joseph S. "The Catcher Takes the Field: Holden, Hollywood, and the Making of a Mann." In Steed, ed. *New Essays*. 79–99.

Way, Brian. "'Franny and Zooey' and J. D. Salinger." *New Left Review* (May–June 1962), pp. 72–82.

Weinberg, Helen. "J. D. Salinger's Holden and Seymour and the Spiritual Activist Hero." In Bloom, ed. *Modern Critical Views*. 63–79.

Wenke, John. *J. D. Salinger: A Study of the Short Fiction*. Boston: Twayne, 1991.

———. "Sergeant X, Esmé, and the Meaning of Words." *Studies in Short Fiction* 18.3 (Summer 1981), pp. 251–259.

Whitfield, Stephen J. "Cherished and Cursed: Toward a Social History of *The Catcher in the Rye*." In Bloom, ed. *Bloom's BioCritiques*. 77–105. Philadelphia: Chelsea House, 2002.

Wiegand, William. "J. D. Salinger: Seventy-Eight Bananas." In Grunwald, ed. *Salinger*. 123–136. New York: Harper and Row, 1962.

Index

Page numbers in **boldface** are illustrations, tables, and charts. Proper names of fictional characters are shown by (C).

About The Author

Raychel Haugrud Reiff, a Professor of English at the University of Wisconsin-Superior, has published fifteen articles on literary topics and effective teaching techniques in various journals and books. Her other books in Marshall Cavendish Benchmark's Writers and Their Works series are *Herman Melville: Moby Dick and Other Works* and *Charlotte Brontë: Jane Eyre and Villette.* She lives in Superior, Wisconsin.